ACTOR'S EDITION

THE TAO OF SHOW BUSINESS

How to Pursue Your Dream Without Losing Your Mind

Debbie,
To your success
Dallas

DALLAS TRAVERS

The Tao of Show Business: How to Pursue Your Dream
Without Losing Your Mind (Actor's Edition)

Published by:
Love Your Life Publishing
PO Box 2, Dallastown, PA 17313
www.LoveYourLifeBooks.com

ISBN: 978-0-9820477-2-9
Library of Congress Control No: 2008943764

Cover design, layout and typesetting by
Cyanotype Book Architects

Printed in the United States of America
Printed on recycled paper.

Praise for *The Tao of Show Business*

"An important key to success as an actor has less to do with talent and craft, and much more to do with the mindset with which we approach our business. Dallas Travers provides an excellent system of tools, perspectives, and practical mechanisms for confronting many of the challenges of making a living as a professional actor."

—Wendy Worthington, actress, *Changeling, Desperate Housewives*

"An inspiring, passionate, and humorous approach to experiencing success inside and out. This book is a must-read for serious actors who are ready to work."

—Joe Palese, director and acting coach, The Actor Space

"Each page in this book outlines practical tools and new insights for actors at every stage in their careers."

—Jay Silverman, Director, Executive Producer, *The Cleaner*

"Many acting books offer little more than how-to strategies. The Tao of Show Business *gives every actor the chance to think differently and take on the business in a whole new way."*

—Miata Edoga, President & Founder, Abundance Bound Inc.

"The Tao of Show Business *is the perfect kick in the pants for actors who want to transform their careers and change their lives. Not only is this book chock-full of easy-to-use tools, but it's thoughtful, comprehensive, and funny!"*

—Mark Rosman, Director, *A Cinderella Story, Ghost Whisperer*

acknowledgements

Ann Christine and Celia Finkelstein are rock stars!
Thank you both for your acute attention to detail.
You, smarty-pants, you!

Thank you to Nick Somers for bringing
The Tao of Show Business to cyberspace.

Christine Kloser—thanks for your guidance.
Love Your Life Publishing brought my vision to the page.

Tiffany, thank you for taking care of business.

And finally…
This book would not be possible without the love,
support, and superstar editing skills of my hubby.
Andrew, you're the greatest.

dedication

A very special thank you to all of the talented actors and artists I've had the privilege of teaching over the course of my career.
Each of you has inspired me to be a better coach
and to continue to live my own Tao.
This book is for you.

This book is for the actors who packed their bags and made the move to Los Angeles or New York in pursuit of a dream.

It's for every actor who deals with the rejection that inevitably comes when you put yourself out there day in and day out.

This book is for every actor who stopped waiting to be hired and started generating work on their own.

It's also for every actor smart enough to ask for help.

This book is for the actors that train to perfect their craft, and who attend workshops and networking events.

It's for the actors who share what they know with their peers.

This book is for every actor who has ever worked for free and for those who might feel a little stuck.

This book is for the actors who love acting and inspire me with their gifts, their talents, and their guts.

This book is for you.

contents

This book contains a few stories from some of the many actors I've had the privilege to coach.

Though their stories are true, I've changed their names to protect their privacy.

first things first...

I invite you to put what you read here into action. To help you do that, I've created *The Tao of Show Business Companion Workbook*. It's my gift to you. Now, you'll have a place to apply what you've learned and gather your thoughts as you discover your own *Tao of Show Business*.

Please visit www.taoofshowbusiness.com/workbook.php to download and print your free companion workbook right now.

Enjoy!

INTRODUCTION: THE WAY IS YOURS

In the sixth century, BC, a Chinese philosopher named Lao Tzu wrote a book called the *Tao Te Ching*. In it, he described *The Tao*, which means "*The Way.*" Boiled down to its most basic terms, the Tao is a simple yet somehow indefinable path to joy for every person who lives according to it.

The Tao is difficult to define because *the way* is different for each and every person. Lao Tzu just offered tools and insight for his readers to utilize so they might discover the Tao for themselves.

It's my intention to do the same for actors through *The Tao of Show Business.* Trust me, I am not a guru or spiritual master, but I have learned a thing or two during my time as an actor's advocate and Creative Career Coach.

Lao Tzu did not believe in stringent rules, regrets or suffering. Instead, he embraced the natural ebb and flow of life. He believed that in order to truly experience happiness, all that humans have to do is live in harmony with the world around them. According to Lao Tzu, happiness exists everywhere, everyday. Humans do not need to struggle in this life in order to enjoy peace in the afterlife.

When you cooperate with life, you will appreciate your journey more fully and experience the true meaning of bliss. You will also experience the joy of acting success regardless of where you are in your career. You do not have to suffer or struggle for years before the big pay-off. You don't need an Oscar before you can celebrate. You can thrive today and start having some fun.

The Tao of Show Business sounds like an oxymoron. In some ways, I suppose it is. At the same time, it's an appropriate definition of an actor's journey in the entertainment industry.

Many people describe this business as crazy and confusing. Let's face it—there truly is no business like show business. Perhaps your job as an actor is not to make sense of the business, rather to make sense of your unique place in it.

Though the entertainment industry is full of rules, recommendations, and recipes for success, every actor's journey is unique. Only you know how to master your own version of success. Only you know what works for you.

There is a way to acting success. With this book as your roadmap, you can blaze your own unique path and live the acting career of your dreams.

The way is yours.

In order to create your own success and live the life you desire as an actor, you must first understand what success means to you and what that picture looks like. You've got to know where you are going before you can get there, right? Living *The Tao of Show Business* means to live in harmony with your own journey as an actor. No one can define success for you. You must do it for yourself and live according to that definition each and every day.

Even while you're on your way to landing a series or starring in that brilliant feature film, it's possible to live a fulfilled and inspired life. Paint a crystal-clear picture of what you want for your career and take consistent action to turn that vision into reality right now. Part one of *The Tao of Show Business* explains the importance of visualizing and describing the vision for your life and for your career.

In Paris, France, back in 1968, an 18-year-old street performer named Philippe Petit found his dream. Sitting in his dentist's office, Petit read an article about the construction of the World Trade Center in New York City; two towers that would one day become the tallest man-made structure in the world. His heart began to race as he realized that he was meant to walk a tightrope across the top of these yet-to-be-built towers.

You see, from a very young age, our friend Philippe always loved to take risks and explore. As a kid, he could often be found climbing trees or running around creating various forms of mischief. This love of adventure and rule breaking carried Philippe into adulthood where he thrived as a pickpocket, street performer, and tightrope walker with multiple arrests around the globe.

Seeing the article and drawing of the Twin Towers was all Philippe needed to identify the specific vision of his purpose. Even though the towers were not yet built, Philippe knew that he would one day connect the two buildings in what he referred to as "le coupe."

During the next six years as the towers underwent construction, Philippe prepared for "le coupe." He devoted his time to perfecting his skills as a high-wire artist, designing and testing all the necessary equipment for the walk, forming the perfect team of accomplices and learning everything he could about the World Trade Center. He also flew to New York twice maneuvering through security to scout the towers, posing as a journalist, a construction worker and even a disabled tourist.

The night before his famous tightrope walk, Philippe and some friends snuck into the towers to complete the mission. While one group made its way up the North Tower, Petit and two friends slipped up to the top of the South Tower. They carried with them a disassembled balancing pole, rigging wires and equipment, 250 feet of one-inch braided steel cable, and a bow and arrow.

They waited in the dark for hours as the buildings fell silent. Finally, Philippe and crew began rigging the rope. The first obstacle was getting the rope from one rooftop to the other. So they shot an arrow tied to fishing line, tied to rope, tied to the tightrope cable itself from the South Tower to the north one. Though they encountered a few challenges, the crew was finally able to secure the steel cable a quarter of a mile in the sky across the 130-foot gap separating the towers.

On the morning of August 7, 1976, Philippe Petit walked out onto his 5/8-inch thick tightrope just as the sun rose. Within moments, Philippe knew he was living out his purpose. Now it was time to enjoy the ride, so he ended up walking, dancing, and even hopping back and forth on that wire, 1362 feet above the busy street below, for nearly an hour.

In the 2008 film, "Man on Wire," Philippe Petit shared his thoughts as he first walked out onto that tightrope. First, Philippe appreciated the brevity and dangerous nature of his coupe. He understood that with each step he took, he could actually lose his life. Yet he believed so strongly that the ideal way to die is to do so having lived your purpose. His purpose was walking that rope. Secondly, Petit realized that he'd been "walking the rope" his entire life. Every action he took led him to his purpose. He was so committed to living his life according to his vision, values, and goals that everything he did reflected who he was and what he stood for. His goal was so clear in his mind and so important to him that nothing at all stood between this man and his dream. Philippe actually said that those forty-five minutes up on that high wire were the easiest and most fulfilling moments of his life.

You, too, have your own version of a tightrope. In order to make your own incredible walk, you must paint the ideal picture of what you want for your life, align that image with your values, and then design a plan of action.

CHAPTER 1: CREATE YOUR LONG-TERM VISION

I MEET A LOT OF ACTORS WHO TELL ME, "I JUST WANNA work." Okay, I get it. As an artist, nothing is greater than having the opportunity to flex your acting muscles and create. But there's a big difference between booking a recurring role on a great series and slaving away on a no-pay, poorly organized independent film that doesn't feed you, let alone ever provide you with footage for your demo reel.

This may seem simple, but you cannot get what you want unless you know specifically what *it* is. It's pretty tough to accomplish something you can't define. So let's drop this "just wanna work" thing and get specific about the direction you want your career to go. Specifically defining your long-term vision will motivate you into action. It will allow you to be curious about your journey. And it'll provide an environment where you can hold yourself accountable to the vision you create.

When it comes to your acting career, what is your "tightrope?" What is that motivating factor that propels you into action? What is your ideal career scene and how does that picture affect the other aspects of your life? When I say ideal, I really mean it. Don't shy away from painting an extraordinary picture of what you really truly want your life and your career to look like. If your ideal scene involves winning an Oscar, the worst thing that will happen is that you'll get close… not too shabby, huh? So go ahead and ask yourself, "What would you do if you knew you could not fail?"

For Philippe Petit, the long-term vision was his World Trade Center walk. This vision was clear, specific, and exciting for him. Long before the towers were even built, Philippe knew in his heart and mind what walking the rope would look like and feel like. This vision stood so firmly in his mind that he had no choice but to take consistent action each day in order to achieve his deepest desire. You must describe the picture of your long-term career vision. This picture must be specific, purpose-filled, and exciting. So exciting in fact, that it forces you to take action each and every day, just like good ol' Philippe.

It's important to remember that your long-term vision is just a measuring stick. Its purpose is to get your blood flowing and to inspire you to take action each and every day. So, don't get too concerned with how you will arrive at this ideal scene; just paint the picture. And paint a specific picture. Allow your senses to experience every detail of your long-term vision. The more specific and clear you make your picture, the more inspired you will become, and the more actions you'll be willing to take. Trust me, if your long-term vision involves working with Ron Howard, you can still be happy and fulfilled if you end up working with Steven Spielberg instead. Ron Howard just represents the type of director with whom you want to work. Allow yourself to paint a very specific picture and trust that your career will unfold in remarkable ways. Often, it ends up being significantly better than what you could imagine for yourself. Just paint the picture and commit to it.

Let's Talk About Commitment

I love this word. It signifies a strong intention and a purposeful goal that has become a part of your being. Commitment manifests as a clear connection to a greater purpose partnered with the sincere desire to take actions in line with that purpose. Commitment is long-term. Commitment is as much about the journey as it is about the result. Commitment is steadfast and solid. It is not a hope or a wish. It is not dependent on any outside person or act. Commitment comes from within. It drives you, it inspires, and it outlasts any obstacle. Commitment is the driving force behind bringing your long-term vision to fruition.

In order to walk your rope, you must commit to every step of the journey without getting too attached to how it all unfolds. What the heck is that supposed to mean, you ask? Good question.

Philippe Petit stayed committed to the Trade Center walk. So committed, in fact that he was willing to experiment and stay curious about how exactly "le coupe" would come together. Shooting the wire from rooftop to rooftop via bow and arrow was not his first idea. He tried several other things before the bow and arrow idea came along. Tons of unexpected changes occurred during the preparation for his walk. The team members changed, the date of the walk was pushed back, and even the rigging equipment even malfunctioned. You name it – it changed. But Philippe knew he was meant to walk the rope across the Twin Towers. He stayed committed to that vision while remaining open and flexible about how exactly it would all come together. Imagine if he had stayed stubbornly attached to any one element of his dream.

When you attach yourself too tightly to how you will bring your long-term vision to life, you run the risk of strangling that very dream to death. On the other hand, when you commit to it, you simply hold the space for your dream to blossom. Attachment is a clenched fist, clinging desperately to whatever small element might be within your grasp, while commitment is an open palm ready to catch whatever miracles come your way. Attachment focuses too closely on how your dreams may come true, while commitment supports the vision itself with no concern about the ever-changing journey. You can't catch anything with a closed fist, so release your attachment to how your dreams will become reality and simply commit to the vision of your ideal scene and move toward that vision every single day.

DESCRIBE THE TAO

Complete the Long-Term Vision Assignment in your *The Tao of Show Business Companion Workbook.*

www.taoofshowbusiness.com/workbook.php

Rely on Your Values

One beautiful thing about Hollywood is that no specific recipe for success exists. Sure, people have opinions about how to pursue a career, but no one knows for certain what's right for you. With so many options and no clear path to success, it's easy to feel overwhelmed and confused about where to begin. But begin you must. You've got to step out onto your tightrope, put one foot in front of the other, and keep on moving forward.

Set yourself up for success by connecting to your values while you pursue your dreams. Your values are those core beliefs or priorities you hold dear. When you take the time to connect to them in order to realize your dreams, nothing will prevent you from eventually accomplishing all that you desire. Values allow you to truly create and maintain momentum during the ups and downs of your career pursuits. Relying on your values also allows you to easily manage your time as well as combat those daily distractions that so often get in your way.

Philippe Petit valued adventure, so he challenged his physical body and mental concentration while training for his Twin Tower walk. He valued risk-taking, so he chose a seemingly impossible location for his coupe. He also valued teamwork, so he enlisted the advice, support and help from his friends. Without his team, the walk would not have happened. Philippe knew his core values and planned every action according to them. He realized his dream because the clarity of his values helped him to move forward.

Knowing and relying on your values provides you with a deeper sense of purpose and reminds you of the big picture. Your values allow you to remain committed to your long-term vision without getting distracted or discouraged by any short-term successes or failures.

Let's say you value financial freedom and you decide that one way to earn great money is through commercial work. With your value of financial freedom in mind, you set a goal to book a national commercial. Yeah, the commercial itself would be great. Think about the money you might make and the fun you might have. So, off you go to book your commercial. After countless auditions and still no booking, you may consider quitting, but because you've tapped into your value of financial freedom, you are willing to continue your pursuit regardless of the rejection you encounter.

Same goes with winning an Oscar. How great would it be to be recognized by the world for all of your hard work, not to mention how cool that little gold statue would look on your coffee table? But the statue is not enough. You must take a look at the shape of your life and the symbolism behind the tangible results you envision. How does winning an Oscar fit into your value system? What does it mean to you? Why is it important?

That's the difference between a value-based goal and a desire-based goal. Goals originating from your values stand the test of time, while goals originating from your thoughts or desires easily fade away when the going gets tough.

Perhaps booking a national commercial will afford you the extra money to invest in retirement, bringing with it a strong sense of security. Maybe winning the Oscar will give you the freedom to finally pick and choose from any number of projects, bringing with it a new sense of freedom.

Consider your own values. What matters most in your life today? Why do you love acting enough to devote yourself to this pursuit? How can you use your values and priorities to create momentum and fulfillment along your career path?

DESCRIBE THE TAO

Tap into your values and consider the Values Appraisal Assignment in your *The Tao of Show Business Companion Workbook.*

www.taoofshowbusiness.com/workbook.php

SELECT A SHORT-TERM GOAL

Once you've painted a clear and exciting picture of your long-term vision and have tapped into your values, it's time to identify possible short-term goals in line with this vision. Remember, there is no clear path to success in Hollywood. Your journey can take any shape, which means that the next step can be anything you choose. Don't worry about making a wrong choice. The only mistake possible would be to do nothing. No one thing you do will make or break you, so just select a short-term goal that inspires you and takes you one step closer to your long-term vision.

Take a look at your long-term vision and brainstorm as many possible short-term goals as you can for a good five or ten minutes. Don't edit yourself here. Just be open and curious about whatever possible ideas come to mind. Heck, why not even try to come up with bad ideas, or better yet the worst possible ideas! I wonder just how awful your ideas could actually get! The point is to allow yourself to come up with the wrong ideas in order to then find the right ones. Just brainstorm. After your brainstorming session, select one to three ideas that most excite you. Ta-Dah! There you have it – your short-term goals. It's really that simple.

Every good goal has four specific elements, so as you clarify your short-term goals be certain they are what I like to call Sage Goals. A Sage is someone respected for his or her wisdom, practicality, and experience, so a Sage Goal must be specific, achievable, genuine, and expansive.

Specific

I know I mentioned it earlier, but one of the easiest mistakes to make as an actor is to set ambiguous or general goals. Ambiguity creates resistance because you are unsure of the steps you must take. Ambiguity makes it impossible to measure your progress because you don't know where the finish line is or how close you are to getting there. Ambiguity does not serve you.

The more specific and clear you can make your short-tem goal, the more specific and clear your path will be. Specificity is a powerful thing. It's one of the greatest motivators and sources of inspiration while you're out there pursuing your dream. Specificity serves as a measuring stick. If you want to make money as an actor, how much money do you want to make? Do you want to make it as an extra or the lead in a successful series? If you want to expand your industry relationships, with whom, specifically, do you want to meet? How many people? What precisely do you want the relationship to look like? Get crystal clear about where you're going so you'll know how to get there.

There is a thin line between being specific and limiting yourself, so be careful. Specificity works to motivate you, not discourage or limit you. Be specific enough to catapult yourself into inspired action without limiting yourself or getting mired down in the minute details. Remember, *The Tao of Show Business* is about enjoying your journey, so be specific yet open to new possibilities. Do not become so stubborn that you remove any chance of fun or fulfillment.

Achievable

A short-term goal is achievable when you believe it is. Really, it's that simple. You must believe that what you desire is truly possible. If you don't believe in it, what's the point in pursuing it?

Okay all you perfectionists out there… listen up! I know you think you're just keeping high standards for your life when you set these super-high expectations for yourself. You're not fooling anyone. You're just falling victim to the most cunning form of resistance I know and it's called perfectionism. Let me tell you something. There is no such thing as perfect. It isn't real, so give it up. When you set a goal that's too far out of reach, the only thing you are doing is setting yourself up for failure and giving yourself an excuse not to really go for it. I'm not telling you to play it safe, but I am suggesting that you commit to creating consistent momentum over the long haul by setting and reaching incremental goals in order to realize your long-term vision one day. In order to lose fifty pounds, you must first lose one, then two pounds, and then a few more pounds. Eventually, you will indeed lose all fifty pounds, but to expect yourself to do it overnight insures disappointment and failure. This is true for your acting career as well. It doesn't make sense to assume that you're going to be an overnight success. Outline achievable short-term goals so that your success will come, not overnight, but perhaps over a few short years. Don't fall victim to your own perfectionism and impatience. Release your high expectations of yourself and replace them with divine desires for your life.

When it comes to your goals, do you truly believe that one day you will accomplish them or do you only wish for them? When you wish for something, it's out of your control and you are separate from it. Wishing leads to wishy-washy actions that lead you nowhere. Stop wishing and start believing that your goals are indeed achievable.

Genuine

Is your short-term goal something you really want? Does it matter enough to you that you're willing to do what it takes to make it happen? If not, your goal isn't genuine and your journey toward achieving it will be long and arduous.

I coached an actor named Brian last year who at nineteen seemed to have his entire career already figured out. Brian saw his long-term vision clearly and he had a plan. Brian's dream career consisted of acting in big summer blockbusters. He looked forward to A-List status and huge box office appeal. Brian's plan was to begin by pursuing commercials. After he booked a couple of those and secured a SAG card, he'd get a contract role on a soap opera and develop a fan base. From there, he'd move into guest starring roles on prime time television eventually moving up to series-regular status, then to starring in his own series. After the series ran for a couple of years, he'd finally make his way into movies and eventually become the action hero he always dreamed of. According to Brian's plan, being an action hero was only about nine years away. Yup. You read correctly - nine whole years.

Though Brian's plan was certainly specific, he felt stuck. His short-term goal was to snag a commercial agent, but he could not motivate himself to take action because frankly, he didn't care at all about booking commercials, starring on a soap, or even having a series. His true desire was to play an action hero in big budget films. That was his purpose, and it didn't include commercial work.

I asked Brian how his pursuits might look different if he only had to pursue the goals he wanted for his career rather than the things he thought were easiest or most likely to happen. Well, Brian hadn't thought of that! After contemplating this new possibility for a few moments, Brian's face lit up and he rattled off dozens of short-term goals much more in line with his long-term vision than his previous plan. He decided to cultivate relationships with directors and producers who typically work on action films. He decided to specifically market himself as an action hero. And he decided to pursue stunt work and independent films. Brian was so excited about these ideas that he was forced to act on them. He began networking with action film directors and producers, creating an action-based demo reel, doing stunt work on films and developing his action hero persona.

Just two years later, Brian booked the lead in an independent action film that got DVD distribution, he auditioned for the lead role in two big budget action features, and his name is currently attached to three other major action flicks. Wouldn't you know it that Brian also booked a couple of commercials, a co-star credit on television, and even a couple of days on a daytime soap opera! Of course he said "yes!" to these opportunities when they arrived, but Brian never took his eyes off the super hero vision that motivated him into action every single day.

Brian is years ahead of schedule because he committed to specific short-term goals directly in line with his long-term vision without worrying about how other actors in the business developed their own careers. His short-term goals were genuinely his, which gave him ownership of his career and kept him moving forward.

Expansive

How does your short-term goal fit into the broader picture of your life? What will you do after you accomplish this short-term goal? Everything you do is connected, so be sure that you know how each step in your career pursuit connects to the next. What's your timeline? Without connecting the dots between each individual short-term goal you cannot maintain consistent momentum. So keep your eyes on the big picture.

Recently, my client named Caroline decided she had to get her house in order before she could take any action toward her acting goals. Her home was in complete disarray, which left her feeling scattered, frustrated, and unmotivated. Caroline knew that the way she treated her house was a direct reflection of the way she approached her career. For many people, cleaning your house has nothing at all to do with making it as an actor. But for Caroline, a messy house was the only block between where she wanted to take her career and the current state of things.

Identify how your short-term goal directly connects to your long-term vision. Connect the dots between today's tasks and tomorrow's results. Doing so will set you up for continuous action and consistent results.

DESCRIBE THE TAO

After you select a short-term goal, identify how that goal meets the four key elements of a Sage Goal.

www.taoofshowbusiness.com/workbook.php

CREATE AN ACTION PLAN

Okay, you know where you want to go. You've brainstormed a bunch of possible next step goals, so now what? Many actors easily become overwhelmed when it comes to creating manageable and tangible plans of action. Though you are clear about where you want to be and pretty clear about where you are right now, the steps between where you are and where you're headed can be pretty foggy.

The Tao of Show Business is a step-by-step process. It's not your job to know precisely how you will reach your long or short-term goals. You aren't required to know every detail of the journey. You must only identify your goal, outline whatever steps you suspect will be required and then begin to take action. With each action comes more information. With more information comes more clarity and decisiveness, allowing you to make your dreams a reality.

Here are three different methods you can rely on to create a practical plan of action to accomplish anything you desire.

Time Traveler

Use this process when you're taking on a large project such as shooting your own film, producing a showcase, creating a demo reel, or designing a marketing campaign.

STEP ONE:	Clearly identify your short-term goal, set a date for completing the entire project, and mark your calendar.

Deadline:	**(March 1st) My new and improved demo reel is completed and hosted online.**

STEP TWO:	Looking at today's date, clearly identify where you are right now in the process.

Today:	**(January 3rd) I have some footage I am proud of, but I need at least one more scene to round out the reel.**
Deadline:	(March 1st) My new and improved demo reel is completed and hosted online.

STEP THREE:	What accomplishments must be completed in order for you to be about fifty percent finished with the project? Describe what halfway might look like and mark this in your calendar on the date exactly halfway between your start date and the projected date of completion.

Today:	(January 3rd) I have some footage I am proud of, but I need at least one more scene to round out the reel.
Halfway:	**(February 1st) Shoot a dramatic scene to add to my demo. Collect the footage from last year's student film project.**
Deadline:	(March 1st) My new and improved demo reel is completed and hosted on-line.

STEP FOUR: Apply the same process in step three to identify your one-quarter-way point (yes, this is a technical term) and mark your calendar accordingly.

Today:	(January 3rd) I have some footage I am proud of, but I need at least one more scene to round out the reel.
One Quarter:	**(January 15th) Select the material and a partner for the scene I will shoot. Begin rehearsals. Review my current material and chose the elements I'd like to add to the final reel.**
Halfway:	(February 1st) Shoot the dramatic scene to add to my demo. Collect the footage from last year's student film project.
Deadline:	(March 1st) My new and improved demo reel is completed and hosted on-line.

STEP FIVE: Do the same for your three-quarter mark.

Today:	(January 3rd) I have some footage I am proud of, but I need at least one more scene to round out the reel.
One Quarter:	(January 15th) Select the material and a partner for the scene I will shoot. Begin rehearsals. Review my current material and chose the elements I'd like to add to the final reel.
Halfway:	(February 1st) Shoot a dramatic scene to add to my demo. Collect the footage from last year's student film project.

Three Quarter:	**(February 15th) Meet with editor to complete reel edits. Send completed reel to web designer for upload. Mail copies of reel to my agent, manager, and mom.**
Deadline:	(March 1st) My new and improved demo reel is completed and hosted on-line.

STEP SIX: Clearly identify what daily, weekly, or specific one-time commitments are required in order to stick with this timeline and move you toward your goal. After you've listed your tasks, prioritize them in order of urgency or importance.

Things to do to stay on track:	**1. Email classmates to find scene partner. 2. Find a scene at Samuel French. 3. Rehearse each week for one hour. 4. Review old footage. 5. Research other reels to identify what works. 6. Consult with agent for suggestions. 7. Update contact information on website.**

By now, you've got a specific timeline and a list of all the small tasks you must accomplish in order to complete your goal on schedule. Decide how much time you can devote to this project each day, schedule it, and get going. You're well on your way to completing your demo reel!

The Time Traveler Technique allows you to avoid falling victim to a feeling of overwhelm. With your timeline in place, you only need to concern yourself with what steps or commitments you need to make in order to take you from your current position to the next stop on your timeline.

DESCRIBE THE TAO

Use the Time Traveler to create an action plan for your short-term goal.

www.taoofshowbusiness.com/workbook.php

The Inch Worm

The Inch Worm action plan process works perfectly for improving those career aspects that are often challenging to measure such as your confidence, your knowledge about the industry, or your craft. The Inch Worm works wonders when the results you hope to accomplish don't necessarily unfold in a linear way. You may want to refer to the Artist Wheel located in your *The Tao of Show Business Companion Workbook* for this one.

STEP ONE: Refer to your Artist Wheel and consider which area of your career you'd like to improve upon. Artist Wheel categories include: craft, finances, confidence, health, creativity, fun, personal relationships, professional relationships, service, spirituality, and personal growth. You may not have a specific goal in mind, but rather an idea about which general area you'd like to focus on. That's quite all right.

STEP TWO: On a scale of 1 to 10, rate your current level of satisfaction in this area. I did not ask you to compare your current situation to your ideal scene. Simply rate how happy you are about where you are right now.

For example, let's say you want one million bucks in the bank. If you compare the $300 you currently have in your bank account to the long-term vision of one million dollars, you'd be forced to rate yourself at a 1 or even zero in the area of finances.

But, if you look at how much your relationship with money has improved lately; how much more responsible you are with your money, the fact that you just received a residual check in the mail, and how confident you are that one day you will indeed be a millionaire, you may rate your level of satisfaction at an 8 or 9 on the scale. So, don't compare your current status to your desired status. Just assess your current level of satisfaction and rate your happiness in this area.

STEP THREE: Now that you've rated your current level of satisfaction, identify what a one or two point improvement might look like. What needs to change in order for your satisfaction in this area to increase?

In the area of finances, you may decide that in order to move from an 8 to a solid 9 you'd like to create a savings plan and stick to it.

STEP FOUR: With a clear picture of what the next number looks like on your scale, identify what actions you must take in order to generate this result.

You might decide to open a Roth IRA account and automatically transfer twenty-five dollars each month toward your retirement.

STEP FIVE: Commit to completing these tasks and schedule the specific time to finish each one.

You could pull out your calendar and schedule your appointment to visit the bank and open your retirement account.

STEP SIX: After you've arrived at the next level on your scale, refer back to step three and repeat this process until you've inched your way to your ultimate long-term goal.

Though the Inch Worm may seem over-simplified, it's an incredible way to maintain consistent and tangible progress when the goal you're striving for seems vague, overwhelming or difficult to measure. Here's a sample of the Inch Worm in action from an actor named Juan:

1. Artist Wheel Area: Confidence

2. Current level of satisfaction is a solid four. Juan feels confident enough with his craft, though he could experience confidence more consistently when it comes to auditions. He does not feel very confident when it comes to the business side of his career and his networking skills could be better.

3. In order to rate his confidence at a six, Juan would like to maintain his composure every time he auditions and to begin attending networking events at least twice per month.

4. To make this happen, Juan commits to joining the networking group his classmate, Sharon, attends. He also schedules fifteen minutes of cold-reading practice each day and begins consistently self-submitting on two casting websites to get more audition practice. Lastly, Juan writes a list of those people he knows that appear to possess the kind of confidence Juan aspires to. Over the next few weeks, Juan takes each one of them out for coffee just to talk about how confidence plays a role in their lives. Nice thinkin', Juan!

5. After keeping to the schedule he created, Juan checks in on his Artist Wheel four weeks later and sure enough, he's more confident about his confidence. Now that he rates himself at a six in this area, he sets the wheels in motion to bring his rating up to an eight.

DESCRIBE THE TAO

Review the Artist Wheel in your *The Tao of Show Business Companion Workbook*. Use the Inch Worm technique to improve those tough-to-measure aspects of your career.

www.taoofshowbusiness.com/workbook.php

Possibility Web

Use the Possibility Web technique when you feel paralyzed by fear, potential disappointment, or a lack of knowledge and know-how. This process also works like a charm when you do not have control over the ultimate outcome such as landing an agent, booking a job, or winning an award. Though the results are not completely up to you, the steps are.

On your journey to success, you will inevitably meet up with some obstacles. But these roadblocks, hiccups, bumps, brick walls, or devastating blows don't have to prevent you from living the career you desire. Many actors (or people in general for that matter) believe that the only way to get what they want is to first overcome the obstacles in front of them. This focuses your energy on the problem rather than your desire. What if getting what you want was actually as easy as adjusting your focus? It can be, if you let it.

A problem only exists if you decide it does. If you take an obstacle and multiply it by zero, you get nothing. In other words, when you choose to do nothing at all to the obstacle, you give it no power and it ceases to exist.

The Possibility Web prevents you from being distracted by

what's in your way and allows you to focus on what might be possible instead. Now you can keep on truckin' toward accomplishing your fullest potential.

STEP ONE: Put your blocks in a box. With your goal in mind, write down each and every thing that prevents you from attaining what you want.

For example, your goal may be to book a speaking role in a big budget feature film. Your list of obstacles might look something like this:

You don't have a SAG card.
You need more training.
Your agent sucks.
You don't have enough time.

No wonder you're stuck! I'm depressed just looking at this list of limitations. After you've listed your obstacles, grab a big fat marker and draw a box around your list. Now draw an enormous and super-strong lock on that thing and lose the combination immediately! You can choose to multiply these obstacles by zero and release any concerns around them. With your blocks all boxed up with nowhere to go, you are free to focus on possibilities.

STEP TWO: Now, with your blocks neatly tucked away, ask yourself an opposite question connected to the possibilities that exist when the obstacle disappears. These questions will free you up immediately and open your mind to many new ideas, emotions, and actions that didn't appear when your focus was on eliminating the obstacle. Here's what I mean:

What would you do if a SAG card didn't matter?
What if your acting chops were ready today?
What if you don't really need this agent to get work?
What would you do if you actually had time?

STEP THREE: Think outside of the box and answer your questions. What would you do if you knew you could not fail? What would you do if obstacles were replaced by possibilities? Write your answers down and create a web of possibility around the lock box. Remember, your goal is to brainstorm in order to find motivation and new ideas, so don't edit.

If a SAG card didn't matter, you would stop worrying about it so much and just pursue the work.

If your chops were ready, you'd start attending casting director workshops and finally register for that showcase you've been meaning to attend.

If you didn't need an agent, you'd start acting like your own agent by pitching yourself, crashing auditions, and rubbing elbows at charity and networking events. You'd drop your headshot and résumé off to other agents and mangers in town and, surely, you'd fire your current agent.

If you had time, you'd work at least one hour each day at perfecting your marketing tools and treating your acting business with the respect that it deserves. You'd stop watching so much reality television and begin working on that web series you wrote last year. You'd get up a little earlier each morning. You'd relax about time in general and have more fun.

STEP FOUR: Draw straws and be daring. Take a look at the possibilities you just created by answering the opposite questions. Select the two or three ideas that stand out or inspire you. Sha-zam! It looks like you've got some short-term goals on your hands. Now brainstorm what actions you can take to turn these possibilities into your reality.

STEP FIVE: Refer back to the Time Traveler process and create a specific timeline for these goals. Got it? Good. Now, go get it!

DESCRIBE THE TAO

Try the Possibility Web on for size and watch the new ideas and inspiration unfold when you switch your focus from obstacle to opportunity.

www.taoofshowbusiness.com/workbook.php

If you have not yet mastered the art of predicting the future, it may be useful to know that life rarely unfolds precisely according to your action plan. So don't feel crazy if you don't quite know every single step required to take you from where you are today to winning an Oscar. The purpose of any action plan is to create accountability and a structure for fulfillment. Use your action plan as a tool to keep you on track. There's no need to get hung up on your action plan or stressed out about each individual step. Just create enough of a plan to get yourself moving, and trust that your plan will unfold as you move forward toward your goals. Try these systems out and see what ultimately works best for you. Just remember the Tao. Describe your vision, identify your goals, create a plan of action, and keep moving. The rest is a piece of cake.

An Inside Job

The Tao of Show Business requires balancing your physical actions with your emotional focus and personal development. It's the dance of art and business. After all of that moving and shaking you've done with your action plans, it's important to show your inner artist some love. Creating a Vision Board is just what the doctor ordered.

You can design a Vision Board to create a physical representation of your ideal scene. Vision Boards allow you to use your artistic skills and creativity and play with the physical picture of your future. They're a lot of fun to make and an effective way to supplement your actions with internal focus. Here's how to create a Vision Board:

STEP ONE: Purchase a large poster board in whatever color you like. Also pick up a glue stick and a pair of scissors while you're at it.

STEP TWO: Gather an assortment of old magazines, pictures, catalogs, and snap shots. You can even print out dynamic or meaningful words that inspire you.

STEP THREE: Take some time and create a space where you can relax and have fun. Creating your Vision Board should be a fun and fulfilling experience. Feel free to pour yourself a beverage, light a candle, or play some music that speaks to you. Now relax, breathe deeply, close your eyes, and imagine the goal you wish to achieve.

STEP FOUR: With your vision clearly defined in your mind, explore how each area of your life and career is impacted by this vision. Think about the twelve areas of the Artist Wheel including craft, finances, marketing tools, relationships, fun, health, creativity, personal growth, spirituality, service and confidence.

STEP FIVE: Now open your eyes and begin to flip through the magazines. Tear out any pictures, words, phrases, and thoughts that inspire you. Don't think about it too much. Simply go through the magazines and remove anything that grabs your attention and inspires you.

STEP SIX: Take your time. Give yourself a few hours or an evening to do this project. After you feel you've reached a stopping point, use the scissors and cut out the words and images you've selected.

STEP SEVEN: After you have cut out the pictures, phrases, and other meaningful images, glue or paste them on your poster board. Reserve space on your board for each area of the Artist Wheel and be sure to place a picture of yourself (one you love to look at) in the center of the board. Feel free to use the Vision Board Grid located in your *The Tao of Show Business Companion Workbook*.

STEP EIGHT: Once your board is completed, put it in a place that you can look at it often. As time passes, feel free to add to your board, or paste over what doesn't work. Make it come alive by dwelling on it for a moment each day. You could make it the first thing you look at in the morning, and the last thing you see before going to sleep. As you concentrate on these visual images, inhale the sensation of having exactly what you want.

DESCRIBE THE TAO

Have some fun making your very own Vision Board! Use the Vision Board Grid in your *The Tao of Show Business Companion Workbook* as a guide.

www.taoofshowbusiness.com/workbook.php

LOSE YOUR LIMITING BELIEFS

The entertainment industry is tough. You have to know somebody in order to be somebody. It takes money to make money. If you're over thirty and haven't made it, you never will. You must be SAG before you can secure an agent and you need an agent before you can get the work that will allow you to become SAG in the first place. Artists are meant to starve. Actors are broke most of the time. Thin is in.

Sound familiar? These are just a handful of so-called rules circulating around Hollywood that poison the minds of even the most logical and practical people in the business. Who says a thirty-something can't make it? Ever hear of a guy named Harrison Ford? He didn't get his break in American Graffiti until he was thirty-one. Then there's Robert Duvall, who was forty-one when "The Godfather" premiered.

Does it really take money to make money? I coached an actor who shot his own short film on his digital camera and went on to sell the project as a feature and make the big bucks. Do you really have to be a member of SAG before you can book TV work? Just today, my student booked a SAG job on a WB pilot. He wasn't a member of the union yet, so the casting director took care of it and provided him with his Taft Hartley waiver. Easy Breezy!

Perhaps you don't have to know somebody in order to catch a break. Maybe it is actually possible to become successful just because you're talented and hard working. Artists can thrive as easily as they can starve and thin is only as in as you want it to be, folks.

Any belief requires mental acceptance. When you believe something, you've just decided to agree with an idea. It's nothing more and nothing less than that. Beliefs are just thoughts that become accepted as facts over time, regardless of their accuracy.

Limiting beliefs are those ideas you've accepted that don't serve you. They're just excuses or fancy thoughts that allow you to avoid truly showing up for yourself. If a belief requires mental acceptance, you can decide for yourself what beliefs you choose to accept.

So, if you don't have any hot Hollywood connections, it doesn't serve you to believe that you must before you can make it as an actor. If you're thirty-eight years old, why on earth would you choose to believe the myth that age matters anyway? Why not instead believe that you are as connected as you need to be and the perfect age to pursue your dream? Regardless of which beliefs you choose to accept, you're just handpicking your thoughts. So why not select the thoughts that support you?

Now is the time to identify those things you believe that may not support the life you desire and drop them like a bad habit!

Your thoughts and beliefs frame every action you take and with the right beliefs you can quickly generate any result you desire. Replace your limiting beliefs with inspired thoughts to literally transform your career overnight. I bet you've got some limiting beliefs that you could do without, so let me show you how to transform them into inspiring choices that work for you rather than limit you.

STEP ONE: Identify your limiting beliefs. Take a good, honest look at those so-called rules you've been buying into and write down which ones don't really work for you.

STEP TWO: Explore how these beliefs support you. You wouldn't be hanging on to them if they weren't serving you in some way.

Perhaps believing that you must be SAG before you can secure an agent saves you from possible rejection or disappointment. Perhaps believing that it takes money to make money protects you from really taking bold risks in your career. Maybe the belief that artists must starve takes you off the hook from living responsibly when it comes to money.

When you really look at how your limiting beliefs serve you, you'll notice that they work to protect you from some fear you've been holding such as rejection, disappointment, failure, success or struggle.

STEP THREE: Now ask yourself how your limiting beliefs have negatively affected you. How do you feel when you believe that this business is tough? How do you feel when you agree that it takes money to make money? Though these beliefs protect you from what scares you, they also prevent you from accomplishing what you desire and make you feel powerless over your career. Yikes!

STEP FOUR: Next, explore who you might be without these beliefs. How would you behave differently? What would change in your career or in your life if you let these beliefs go?

Without the belief that you need an agent in order to get any acting work, you could choose to actively pursue the work yourself.

Without the belief that you're not thin enough to be hired, you just might be someone who books work because you're not only talented, but you're the perfect size just as you are. Without your limiting beliefs, you'd not only be in hot pursuit of the career of your dreams, you'd actually be living it!

STEP FIVE: Live without these beliefs. Really, just put them away for a while. You can go grab them later if you want. Take a week and pretend you no longer believe these thoughts. Just set them aside and explore what life might be like without your limiting beliefs. Through this, you will liberate yourself and discover that your limiting beliefs weren't actually true in the first place.

DESCRIBE THE TAO

Complete the Limiting Beliefs exercise in your *The Tao of Show Business Workbook* and live for one week without those beliefs.

www.taoofshowbusiness.com/workbook.php

Whether you think you can or you think you can't accomplish the vision you've set for yourself, you are probably right. So why not believe you can and behave that way every day? Though you can't control when you'll catch your big break, you can plan for it, paint the picture and truly believe that it's possible for you. You can master *The Tao of Show Business.* You can do so by releasing your limiting beliefs and embracing an empowered attitude.

Charles Swindoll once wrote in his book, *Great Attitudes! 10 Choices for Success in Life*, "The longer I live, the more I realize the impact of attitude on life. Attitude, to me, is more important than facts. It is more important than the past, than education, than money, than circumstances, than failures, than successes, than what other people think or say or do. It is more important than appearance, giftedness, or skill. It will make or break a company... a church... a home. The remarkable thing is we have a choice every day regarding the attitude we will embrace for that day. We cannot change our past. We cannot change the fact that people will act in a certain way. We cannot change the inevitable. The only thing we can do is play on the one string we have, and that is our attitude ... I am convinced that life is 10% what happens to me, and 90% how I react to it. And so it is with you... we are in charge of our attitudes."

Declaration is the second key element to *The Tao of Show Business*. After you describe your vision and create a plan of action, it's time to open your mouth and talk about that vision. You cannot get what you want until you are willing and able to actually say the words out loud.

Declaration creates accountability. By expressing your desires to the world, you create the space for those things to meet you. While pursuing an acting career, you are your own boss. No one monitors how often you go to class, self-submit, or send a mailing. You're on your own, but you're not alone. Every time you talk about what you're up to with others, you create a support system that holds you accountable and allows the people who care about you to help you out.

In this section of the book, I'll show you how to easily cultivate powerful relationships so you can network like a pro. I'll teach you how to take a meeting by preparing properly and asking powerful questions. Most importantly, I'll show you how to transform your negative self-talk into empowering beliefs that will allow you to eliminate self-doubt and create amazing career breakthroughs. It's a lot to cover, so let's get started.

Chapter 5: Make Your Goals Public

How often have you set goals or resolutions that you never kept? How often have you attended a class, taken copious notes, yet never put what you learned into action afterward? Have you ever quietly committed to change a habit or behavior and then struggled to actually make the change?

It's pretty tough to generate new results if you don't continuously focus on the change you want to bring about. Resolutions often don't work because you set the goal, write it down and then forget about it. That's also what happens with binders full of notes. Quiet personal promises rarely come to fruition because they don't have room to grow. They're just a secret you keep to yourself.

Your career is a lot like a precious and exotic plant. Let's pretend you've got a one-of-a-kind orchid that's so beautiful it takes your breath away. Now, you don't know a lot about orchids, but you do know that they're fragile and that they require special care and attention. Fearing that your orchid will not survive in the hands of your roommate, your girlfriend, your mom who's in town for the week, or anyone else for that matter, you decide that the only way to keep your orchid intact is to lock it in the cupboard. At least in the cupboard, nobody can get his or her grubby hands on your precious plant! Two weeks later, you remember your orchid and race to the cupboard door. When you open it up, you sadly find the wilted and dry remains of a once beautiful piece of perfection.

Why then do you lock your dreams away, protecting them from the very elements they need to blossom? Your future is just like that precious orchid. It needs exposure to sunlight to grow into its fullest potential. It needs water for hydration, healthy soil for nourishment, fresh air, and room to expand. Let's face it, sometimes your own mother's advice may feel like a hurricane or a nasty bug infestation. Perhaps a fellow actor's negativity may suck the air out of the room. Maybe so-called industry experts will scorch you with their insight on the hardships of Hollywood. It's your job to expose yourself to all of these elements and pay special attention to just how much sunlight, water and wind your little orchid can take. At times, it may be difficult or discouraging, but without these things, your dreams will surely die. Don't keep your goals to yourself. Just like that precious flower, your career deserves to thrive in an expansive environment.

Embrace the power of making your goals public. Go out there and share your plan, talk to people, collect insight and gather support. Your job in this business, above and beyond everything else, is to become known. Nobody gains notoriety by sitting quietly at home watching *Law and Order* reruns.

I am not suggesting that you run around town expressing your desires to everyone you meet on the street. Instead, I urge you to think about your goals often, so that your future vision automatically becomes a part of what you talk about and how you operate every single day. You must become comfortable enough with who you are today and where you're heading tomorrow that you can authentically speak about this journey in any circumstance.

You must be willing to express your desires, share your action plan, and celebrate your successes, free of expectation. Regardless of how others will perceive you or receive your goals, your dreams deserve the opportunity to thrive by being exposed to the elements. I have no doubt that you will encounter many nay-sayers and crazy-makers on your journey to acting success, but you'll also meet your future collaborators, mentors, and supporters. Trust me, it's much easier to generate the results you desire with the help of a team rather than trying to do it solo.

What you say is what you get. If you don't say anything, you'll get nothing. If you sheepishly talk about your acting career only in safe environments after much poking and prodding, expect your goals to be reached just some of the time and only in safe environments. So how willing are you to talk about the career you're creating? How willing are you to share your goals with the people in your life? How willing are you to watch your future bloom right before your eyes?

MASTER THE ART OF POSITIVE SPEAKING

OKAY, BEFORE YOU DIVE INTO DECLARING YOUR CAREER goals to your friends, agents, coaches, and relatives, it's important to first master your self-talk. You must frequently think about, write about, and whisper to yourself your career vision. Doing so will allow your bones and bloodstream to absorb this vision. When your bones feel it, your body will act upon it.

Create the physical connection to your visions. Keep a goal-getting journal where you not only log your daily achievements, but also describe on paper what your long-term vision looks like, tastes like, and feels like. Talk about this vision privately at first and then share it with the people you trust most. If you haven't already done so, complete the Vision Board exercise located in your *The Tao of Show Business Companion Workbook*. Your words are powerful. Use them.

Develop a deeper awareness of the questions you ask yourself. Did you know that the average person has over fifty thousand thoughts per day? Many of these thoughts appear as questions. Most people walk around asking themselves mental questions all day long. Go on and admit it. You talk to yourself every day. It's okay. It's actually normal.

It's important to realize that your life today is a direct reflection of the thoughts you have. The questions you ask yourself impact the way you feel. Your mood and emotions always influence the actions you take and your actions then shape your life.

Your subconscious mind is programmed to affirmatively support the questions you ask it. It will automatically answer your questions and even provide evidence to support the idea you're inquiring about.

So if you ask, "Why do bad things always happen?" your subconscious mind will give you all the reasons why bad things do indeed happen to you.

Don't believe me? Try it. Go ahead and ask yourself, "Why can't I get ahead?" Go on... I'll wait.

Did you notice that your subconscious mind answered you or that your physical body responded with a knot in your stomach, pressure on your shoulders, or an all around icky feeling? That's a common reaction. Your gut is designed to agree with your head. The trouble with that comes when your head asks the wrong questions.

Never fear! There's an easy fix here. If you want to generate new results, the trick is to simply ask yourself different questions or practice what I like to call Living Mantras.

Living Mantras are empowering questions that reflect or support the life you desire. They're powerful, present tense statements about the person you are becoming. When practiced regularly, Living Mantras will not only help you accomplish your career goals, but they'll absolutely transform your life!

Give it a whirl and try asking yourself, "Why am I so lucky?" Again, I'll wait. Really, I don't mind.

Did you notice that your subconscious mind answered that question too? Did you also notice how differently your body responded? It sounds silly, but it works. Your subconscious mind can't help but support the questions you ask it, sparking a positive reaction and jump-starting your progress toward change.

The next time you find yourself at an audition thinking thoughts like, "What if I don't book this?" or "Why am I even here?" Try out the Living Mantra technique and just ask, "What if I book this?" Or, "Why are auditions so easy for me?"

One key element to making Living Mantras work for you is the way you feel when you practice your mantras. You can ask yourself questions all day long about how wonderful your life is, but if you don't feel wonderful, you won't experience the reality of your mantras. You must allow your entire being: body, mind, and soul to experience the feeling of your mantras at work. Remember, when your bones feel it, your body will follow. When it comes to declaring your goals and sharing yourself with others in the industry, Living Mantras allow you to feel happy and confident on the inside enabling you to convey that grounded feeling on the outside.

Creating your own mantras is a piece of cake! Let me show you how to create three types of Living Mantras: Long-Term Vision Mantras, Obstacle Busting Mantras, and Mantras for Immediate Change.

Long-Term Vision Mantras

First, begin with your long-term vision in mind and create Living Mantras that speak specifically to the vision you've created.

Let's say you want to win an Oscar. Imagine what that might be like. Picture yourself winning the Oscar. Picture what you're wearing, the red carpet, the crowd and the acceptance speech. Don't forget to let your bones really feel the sensations around this incredible picture. You could then try long-term vision mantras like:

Why do I always deliver such award-winning performances?
How does my work impact so many people?
Why does everyone try to hold my Oscar?

Be willing to experiment with your mantras until you find the ones that trigger an automatic thrilling response in your body. You might notice that some mantras feel better than others. You'll know when you've found the right ones because they'll make you smile, laugh, relax completely, or even shiver with excitement.

Obstacle Busting Mantras

You can also use Living Mantras to overcome obstacles or break through fears. Let's stick with the Oscar example for a moment. You may feel that before you are ready to win your Oscar, you need more confidence, stronger industry relationships and more opportunities to do film work.

w that you've identified your immediate obstacles, you antras that inspire you to bust through those suckers. removing mantras could be:

When did I become so confident and self-assured?
How is it so easy to meet all the right people?
Why do incredible opportunities always fall in my lap?

Mantras for Immediate Change

Design some other Living Mantras to change specific elements of your current situation. Begin by identifying what you no longer want or what you desire to change. Perhaps you're tired of feeling broke and worrying about money. Maybe you're afraid of failing as an actor.

Often times, what you don't want offers itself in the shape of fear or negative thought. Try not to focus too much energy on your fears or those things you don't want. Sometimes though, the easiest way to identify what you do want is to look at your fears, worries, or negative thoughts.

After you've identified your fears and negative thoughts, you must release any attachment to them. It can be very liberating just say out loud, "I release my fear of not having enough money!" It's even more fun to say this into your open palm, catch those words, ball them up and toss them out the window.

Now replace your fear with a positive declaration such as "I invite wealth and prosperity into my life today."

With this new desire in mind, create some Living Mantras that speak directly to what you desire rather than to what you don't want. Such as, "Why am I so good with my money?" or "Where did all this money come from?'

Again, it's important to explore many possibilities before you find the perfect ones for you. Just remember to play and be curious. Here are a bunch of my favorite Living Mantras. Check 'em out. Pick some of your very own mantras and put them into practice.

Relationships

Why am I so highly respected for the work that I do?
Why are my relationships so fun and fulfilling?
I believe in the power of teamwork.
How is it so easy to connect with all the right people?

Success

Why am I so successful and prosperous?
The entertainment industry is fun & easy!
How is it so easy to be so successful?
Why does success follow me wherever I go?

Confidence

I trust myself to be myself in everything I do.
When did I become so confident and grounded?
Why is it so easy to take risks and grow?
How did I become such a genius?

Wealth & Money

Why does everybody want to give me money all the time?
Where did all of this money come from?
Why do I get paid so much to do what I love?
How did I get so filthy rich?

Booking the Job

Why do I book everything I audition for?
How does great work always fall in my lap!
Why is auditioning so much fun?

Perseverance

How is it so easy to let go of the past?
I am willing to fully experience my own unique journey.
I am right on time, all of the time.
My career unfolds in remarkable ways.

Living Mantras work because they make you feel inspired. When you practice mantras daily, you trigger positive feelings that create inspired actions. These actions then catapult you toward new and exciting results. It begins with putting attention on the thoughts you have and the questions you ask yourself.

Try out some Living Mantras for a couple of weeks. Remember your career today is a direct result of the thoughts you have and the questions you ask yourself. Perhaps it's time to try some new thoughts, ask some different questions and truly master the art of positive speaking. It's worth a try.

DECLARE THE TAO

Write your own Living Mantras in your *The Tao of Show Business Companion Workbook* and practice writing or reciting them for the next thirty days or so.

www.taoofshowbusiness.com/workbook.php

The Tao of Show Business involves clear communication, first with yourself and then to those around you. Declare yourself to be that person today. This successful behavior will inspire even more successful behavior. When you have the courage to live as if everything you desire is truly possible today, you will force yourself to act in a strong, empowered and successful manner, no doubt generating amazing results. It starts with your self-talk.

The way you treat yourself frames the way you communicate with others. Get your self-talk polished up and ready to go so you can step out in the industry and cultivate lasting, powerful relationships.

RELATIONSHIPS: PLANT SOME SEEDS

Your self-talk is stupendous. You feel confident and radiant. You're ready to face the world and declare yourself to be amazing, successful and really talented! Now, it's time to… yes, I'm going to say it… network.

Networking often gets a bad rap. Actors in particular reject networking because it feels fake and tedious while bringing up major insecurities and questions. Nobody likes to schmooze, right? Like it or not though, you must cultivate relationships in order to build a career in this business. You can be the most talented actor in the history of acting, but if nobody knows who you are, you won't have the opportunity to strut your stuff.

In order to really network effectively, the first thing you must do is redefine the word itself. In doing so, you'll reshape your approach to building relationships. Reframe how you perceive networking. Rather than define it as schmoozing, you can view it as cultivating. When you change your perspective, networking quickly becomes a fun way to connect with others rather than a chore. Just remember that when you schmooze, you lose.

While Schmoozers concern themselves with *quantity*, Cultivators care about the *quality* of their relationships. Schmoozers measure success by the size of their Rolodex. Cultivators understand the value of solid relationships. They may know fewer people, but they're known, respected, and trusted by everyone in their circle.

Schmoozers love to name drop. They concern themselves with statistics, impressions, and résumés. Schmoozers hang out at the surface of relationships, never investing in personal connections. Cultivators on the other hand, don't judge others based on credits or credentials alone. They value exploration and personal experiences. Cultivators believe that there is always more than meets the eye and they trust themselves to formulate their own opinions about people they meet.

Schmoozers are often motivated by fear. They guard their secrets and are leery of others. Schmoozers put on shows and throw up walls protecting them from the opinions and insights of others. Cultivators practice openness. They love to share their insight and energy. Cultivators are great listeners and often listen more than they speak.

Schmoozers keep score. They believe in competition and see everyone as a threat. Schmoozers focus on scarcity rather than abundance. They are often disappointed or jealous when those around them experience success. Cultivators understand that there's more than enough to go around. They celebrate the successes of others and appreciate the examples set by their peers. Cultivators don't compete as much as they cooperate. They focus on abundance and never fear losing or being left behind.

Schmoozers are fickle. In relationships, they focus on "me." They struggle to be patient and often give up too soon. Schmoozers view relationships as a chore. Cultivators invest in the long-term when it comes to relationships. They are loyal to those they care about; yet understand that every relationship must be mutually beneficial. Cultivators are happy to give before they receive and always view the relationship as a gift.

By moving away from a Schmoozer mentality and becoming a Cultivator, your networking experiences will transform overnight. Relationship building will feel natural and easy. Plus, it'll be a ton of fun. Now, imagine that you are a master gardener, out there planting seeds, pulling weeds and cultivating healthy crops all the way from Hollywood to Bollywood.

Seed Planting Strategy

It's been said that every super successful person such as Bill Gates, Warren Buffet, Tiger Woods, and the like, was able to achieve greatness because of the help of six key individuals surrounding and supporting them on their career journey. Six key people, not eight million. If this is the case, you no longer have to worry about meeting and knowing everybody in town. You only have to build solid relationships with six key players who can join you on your journey to acting success. When it comes to cultivating, quality trumps quantity every time. It's not about who you know, but about who really knows you. And you don't have to know Jerry Bruckheimer (though I'm sure he's a great guy) in order to have a thriving career. The key is to cultivate solid relationships with the people you already know, as well as the ones you meet in your day-to-day life. Build solid relationships with the people in your life and invite them to join you on your journey to the top.

For all you network-a-phobes out there, here's a simple strategy to help you easily and effortlessly transform networking into cultivating and double your chances of sky-rocketing to the top of your field.

STEP ONE: Attend one cultivating event every month. You could attend casting director workshops, industry breakfasts, film screenings, or plays. You could also attend a friend's barbeque, or a classmate's dinner party. It doesn't have to be an official, stuffy "networking event" in order to count. Just get out of your house and into the company of your future Collaborators.

STEP TWO: Connect with one new person at each event. Really connect with them. The point here is to cultivate meaningful and authentic relationships and you can't do that if you're not willing to listen well and share yourself. Find out who they are, what they're excited about, and where they're headed personally and professionally. Then, it's your job to share the same about who you are, where you're headed, and what you are excited about.

This requires some practice. I'm not suggesting that you fire off questions like, "Who are you? What are you excited about? Where do you see yourself in the next five years?" I'm encouraging you to have a real conversation here. Be interested as well as interesting.

The same goes when talking about yourself. Don't blurt out statistics or name drop. Actually share your experiences. Allow yourself to express your excitement about what's going on in your life right now. If you feel like you have nothing to be excited about, you've got to take a good hard look at what the heck you're doing! You're an actor who's actually pursuing your dream. That alone is exciting and impressive. You're an artist who loves to tell stories and express yourself through film. That's exciting! You're one of the lucky ones. You're brave enough and smart enough to listen to your bones and follow your passion. Get excited about it.

STEP THREE: Set up the follow up. After you've connected with one new person, ask if they'd like to stay in touch. Collect their email address or phone number. Let them know you'd love to have coffee, invite them to a show, or just stay in touch online. Exchange information. Next, be sure to get in touch and stay in touch with this newfound friend. They just might be one of your key six for success. Don't allow too much time to pass before you get in touch. The longer you wait to call or email, the more difficult it will become. Contact your new Collaborator within ten days while you're both still feeling connected.

If you follow these three steps you'll develop twelve solid relationships over just one year. That's twice as many relationships than you need to make it to the top. Cool, huh?

Be great. Be accessible.

As an emerging actor in this business you've got two tasks at hand when it comes to seed planting. You must be great and you must be accessible. Boise Thomas, a very successful commercial actor and coach, believes that a big part of his success can be credited to his ability to just "be great". When Boise says that you must "be great", he means that you must be great in everything you do. You must practice greatness everywhere. It's not enough to be a talented actor who's great in auditions. You must be great in every circumstance. When you practice greatness at your day job, at the Starbucks, while stuck in traffic, and in acting class, people will regard you as great and will want to work with you. Nothing you do is in a vacuum. As the old saying goes, "The way you do anything is the way you ultimately do everything," so just be great.

Naomi, an actress and client of mine, waited tables to support her acting pursuits. Naomi often worked the lunch shift, where weekly regulars had business meetings while they dined. After months of eating in Naomi's section, one regular customer asked her, "So Naomi, what do you do?"

Naomi thought this was an odd question. After all, she was his designated waitress. Then again, many Angelenos wait tables in order to fund their dreams. So, Naomi sheepishly answered, "Well, you know, I guess I'm trying to do the acting thing." Naomi felt shy about admitting she was an actress because she feared others would judge her.

Unimpressed with her answer, the customer proceeded to tell her off. He replied, "Don't apologize for pursuing your dreams. You're great! You're good with people and an excellent waitress. If you're half the actress that you are the waitress, you're bound to be really successful. Now that I finally know you're an actress, I can help you!"

It turns out that this loyal customer just happened to be the VP of Casting at a major television network. He happily referred Naomi to several talent agents and even pulled some strings to get her a co-starring role on a prime time series. You never know how opportunities will present themselves to you, so be great in all that you do. Practice greatness everywhere, so you'll be known as someone who's great and people will love you for it.

Great, you're great. But being great is not enough. You must also be accessible and open to those around you. Being great is one thing, but remember that people have to know how great you are in order to connect with you. Naomi did a great job of being great, but she wasn't very accessible when it came to her acting career. She rarely talked about it and when she did, she totally downplayed her pursuits. Her customer literally had to drag the information out of her. She made it difficult for him to help her out because she was unwilling to be accessible.

Practicing accessibility can feel like a balancing act between being real and being a poser. When you cultivate rather than schmooze though, it's easy to be authentic and accessible. Another client named Vivian struggled to cultivate meaningful relationships. Though Vivian trained regularly, had a handful of indie film credits as well as a couple of co-stars, she feared that people in the industry might judge her as a wanna-be rather than a working actor. So Vivian had a stock answer whenever she met new people. She'd tell them that she was a bartender trying to act. She would continue on saying that unless you have a bizarre affection for crappy horror films that go straight to DVD or awful theatre in Los Angeles, you probably haven't ever seen her work. She may not act much, but she pours a mean gimlet.

By pulling the comedy card, Vivian avoided admitting that she was working hard on her career. She avoided the mockery or judgment of others, but proceeded to mock and judge herself. Worst of all, Vivian avoided becoming known for who she really was and lost countless opportunities to cultivate valuable and fulfilling professional relationships.

Vivian's story is not unique. Many emerging actors fear that others might judge them, reject them, or challenge their validity in the industry. They believe their efforts don't count until they have the credits to match their efforts. Even then, if the credits aren't recognizable network television roles or movies lucky enough to be released, the work still doesn't count.

I don't know who came up with the official definition of what it means to be a working actor, but come on, folks. If you're reading this book, you're working. If you train, self-submit, audition, do shows, research, or take action for your career, you're working. If you have the courage to move away from your family in order to pursue a career, face rejection every time you don't book a job, deal with negative feedback about your talent, your look and your know-how, you're working. Landing a role and working on a set is the easy part. The real work comes way before that stuff.

Trust me, though it may feel easier to play off your acting pursuits as a hobby or some sort of joke, you're not doing yourself any favors. You're not embracing the Tao, and you're not connecting with other people in a way that serves you. Though it may seem like an easy way out, self-deprecating humor isn't the way to go in the long run.

Other actors rattle off all of their industry credits like they're in some sort of credit competition when asked about their work. Motivated by fear, they spend so much energy trying to prove themselves that they miss the point of connecting entirely. They come off as braggarts with a bunch of fancy credits, but no people skills. The people you meet don't care about how much work you've done as much as they care about you, your experiences, your insights and your thoughts about the work you've done. They want to connect with you the person, not you the résumé.

These self-deprecating, defensive, or fearful attitudes will pulverize you whenever you meet new people who just happen to ask the inevitable question, "So, what do you do?" which is often followed by, "Have I seen you in anything?" How often have conversations taken a turn for the worse because you were unable to really own the fact that you're a hard working, talented actor earnestly pursuing a career that many view as tough or even impossible?

I met an archeologist last year. Yeah, I know... a real archeologist. Just like Indiana Jones! It was really cool. I'd never met an archeologist before and I was fascinated! Feeling excited and intrigued, I opened my mouth and said, "Oh, really? I didn't know that was a real job! What does an archeologist do, anyhow?"

Contrary to how it appeared, I wasn't judging this woman or questioning her credentials as a professional. I was actually attempting (lamely, I admit) to connect with her and find out more about her job. She managed my questions gracefully and soon we moved on to an engaging and authentic conversation about our jobs, our travels, and our lives in general. We were able to do this only because she identified my poorly presented question for what it was: an attempt to connect.

Your Concrete Commitment

Think about it. When you meet someone new, don't you usually break the ice with a comment about the weather, the food, or the current state of the world? Don't you then ask them about their job? Don't you then ask more about their job, what it's like, or how they got started? You're not practicing your private detective skills when you ask these questions. You're just trying to connect, right?

It's possible then that when others ask you these same questions that they, too, are attempting to connect with you. When you answer with a joke, an apology, defensiveness, or some other form of shtick, you're not allowing them to connect. You're stopping the conversation cold.

The next time you're asked, "So, what do you do?" Or "What have I seen you in?" Hear the question behind those questions, which is "How can I relate to you?" Now, that's a question you can answer honestly and authentically!

Develop your Concrete Commitment so you can gracefully answer the inevitable questions that come when you meet someone new. Present yourself like the easy-going, charming, talented person you are rather than a weirdo who can't seem to talk about their job. Your Concrete Commitment includes three elements: who you are, what you're excited about, and what's on your horizon.

1. Who are you?

You are so much more than any one thing. Though you love acting and art, it does not define you. A friend of mine used to work for a cruise ship. She'd guide small groups around the ports for a day whenever the ship docked. To break the ice as she started the tour, she would invite her guests to introduce themselves and describe "what they did". Fascinatingly enough, the Americans would answer by discussing their profession while the Europeans answered with their hobbies or other interests. Yes, you are an actor, but you are more than that. Who are you above and beyond that? Remember… be great and be accessible.

2. What are you excited about?

Express yourself and share your enthusiasm. You are lucky enough to be following your passion and it's cool to be excited about it. This is not about bragging, but about being accessible. When you see a great movie, eat at a great restaurant, or read a great book, you're happy to spread the word. Do it for yourself, too. If you're in a slump, that's okay. Just be honest about it. What a relief to be able to openly share that you don't have much going on lately, and admit that you're excited to finally start booking jobs! Be real. It's much more interesting.

3. What's on your horizon?

Perhaps you have a show coming up, maybe you're planning a trip to wine country, or maybe you're learning how to tap dance. This is all interesting and engaging when you allow it to be. Just share what's up and what's next for you.

The best way to be accessible is to also ask great questions. Nobody wants to listen to some yahoo talk about himself all night. Sure, talk about yourself. Share your Concrete Commitment, but don't forget to allow others to do the same. Be mindful of the questions you ask. Rather than using the common question, "So what do you do?" Try asking things like, "What do you like best about your job?" "Is your line of work fulfilling?" or "Tell me more about that!"

Your Concrete Commitment will take some work before it becomes a fit for you, so take the time to practice and develop it. Appreciate the fact that the more you practice sharing your Concrete Commitment, the better you'll be at it. Soon enough, you'll be connecting with new people easily and effortlessly. Be willing to talk about who you are, what you're excited about, and what's on your horizon. Be flexible as you perfect this practice and have fun sharing the real you.

DECLARE THE TAO

Brainstorm and play with your Concrete Commitment. Answer the Concrete Commitment questions in your *The Tao of Show Business Companion Workbook*, then go out there and put it into practice.

www.taoofshowbusiness.com/workbook.php

RELATIONSHIPS: PULL SOME WEEDS

It's natural for weeds to show up in every garden, so plan on it. Plan on meeting some people you just don't click with. Plan on fumbling occasionally through meetings. Plan on falling victim to assumptions and asking the wrong questions. It's part of the Tao, which is the natural flow of your career. These weeds don't have to spoil the entire crop though, so it's your job to identify them and remove those suckers as soon as you can. Every time you pull a weed, you'll become more adept at identifying them and sooner than later you'll be able to avoid them all together.

Collaborators and Sideliners

On your road to success, you are certain to meet tons of people with varying backgrounds, talents, and personalities. I'm pretty sure that along the way, you're gonna click with some people better than others. This is a good thing. Don't worry about impressing everyone. Don't distract yourself by worrying about being liked, hired or accepted. Your job is to simply cultivate relationships with the right people and plant seeds.

In life and especially in the entertainment industry, you'll find two types of people. First, you've got the Collaborators. These people just love you! They want to hire you, represent you, make movies with you, and even take you out to dinner. Collaborators recognize that you are a creative genius. They think you're talented, charming, and easy to work with. These people support the decisions you make, trust your opinions and know your future is a bright one. Simply put, Collaborators are your people.

Next, you've got the Sideliners who really just aren't your people. Regardless of your talent, your weight, your connections, or your work ethic, Sideliners just won't get you. They're not supposed to. The industry is filled with way too many people for you to keep track of, so it's the job of every Sideliner to not be your person. Not everyone is lucky enough to be a Collaborator and the Sideliners just show you where to focus your energy. Maneuvering through the industry becomes a lot easier when you recognize that Sideliners are just doing their job when they criticize you, don't return your calls, reject you, or just rub you the wrong way. It's not about you, or even them for that matter. They're really not your people. They're Sideliners and they're not meant to join your team.

Rather than spin your wheels and spend your time trying to convert the Sideliners, just recognize that they're not your people and thank them for mastering their jobs. This mentality will free you up to focus on the people who matter. Pull your Sideliner weeds. Shift your focus away from the Sideliners and look toward the Collaborators. They're waiting for you.

I have a few Sideliners in my life and I've developed a love affair with every one of them. This was not always the case, though. For years I struggled with a very special Sideliner who happens to work down the hall from my office. Let's call him Albert, shall we? Well, Albert the master Sideliner loves to yell at people. He's a know-it-all who loves to be nosey, bossy, and annoying. Albert also hates to shower and he loves to stink up the place, that's for sure. Albert is clearly not my person. He's a Sideliner through and through.

The first couple of years I knew Albert, I let him drive me insane. When I wasn't arguing with him, I spent too much time wondering, "Why is he like this? Doesn't he get it? What can I do to make him understand?" Who knows how much useless energy I directed at trying to fix a relationship that actually wasn't broken? Nothing was *wrong* with me or with Albert. We just weren't meant to get along.

So I gave up trying to change this person and began embracing his impressive Sideliner skills. I began expecting Albert to behave like Albert who is often bossy, stinky, and nosey.

Things changed immediately. Free of my Sideliner distractions, I began to focus on my business, my clients, and all the fabulous Collaborators in my life. Albert still did his thing, but I was now in charge of what I expected from him. By expecting Albert to be Albert, nothing he did annoyed me any longer. You see, it wasn't Albert who bugged the jeepers out of me; it was my belief that he *should* be a Collaborator.

Today I am happy to report that Albert and I have a great relationship. Some might even call it a friendship of sorts. No, he didn't transform. Nothing changed, really. I simply aligned my expectations with what's true. What's true is that Albert is a Sideliner and to expect anything else is to drive myself batty. By accepting Albert for who he is and expecting him to act exactly as he does, I'm no longer angry or upset when he does his job. Actually, I'm sort of amused by it because Albert is truly one-of-a-kind.

Got any Sideliners hanging around? Perhaps you have an agent who rarely returns your calls and never gets you auditions. No problem! She's just not your agent. Stop wondering why this relationship isn't working out like you thought is should and start looking for the Collaborator who is your agent. Maybe your acting coach rants and raves while you learn nothing new. Easy, breezy! Looks like he's not your coach after all. Worried that your sister doesn't support your career pursuits? Piece of cake! She's still your sister; she's just not in charge of your cheering squad. Allow her to be herself and get support elsewhere.

While you will achieve the ultimate career success with the help of the Collaborators, you may easily become distracted and discouraged by the Sideliners. Don't fall victim to this. The opinions of others are none of your business. The actions of others don't concern you. You are not in charge of anyone else, so stop trying to do everybody's job and mind your own business. Your business involves becoming a successful actor and sharing your gifts with the world. That's a big job and you've got your work cut out for you. Success comes more easily when you accept that, along the way, some people won't be your people. Just know that many, many more will be. That is for certain.

Think about the people in your professional life that may be Sideliners. Don't judge them, try to change them, or even tell them that they're not your people. Just expect them to behave like the Sideliners that they are. They're just doing their job.

DECLARE THE TAO

Free Your Mind! Check out the Sideliner Exercise in your *The Tao of Show Business Companion Workbook.*

www.taoofshowbusiness.com/workbook.php

Ask the Real Question

Sideliners aren't the only ones who create weeds in your Tao Declaration Garden. You can create some hefty weeds all by yourself whenever you operate under assumptions and ask unclear and inaccurate questions. A big part of taking care of your relationships involves asking the real question. Recently, my client Brad secured a meeting with a reputable talent manager. Brad was excited to take the meeting because this manager seemed to be the perfect fit for him. The meeting went beautifully. Brad was charming and at ease. He asked great questions. The manager liked his demo reel and expressed confidence in his future as an actor. After over an hour of talking, getting to know each other, and having a great time, things suddenly got a little weird.

You see, as the meeting ended, Brad assumed that if this manager had interest in representing him, she would tell him so. It makes sense, right? Brad's assumption prevented him from asking the real question, so the meeting slowly puttered to a stop. He left feeling unsure about whether the manager wanted to work with him and unclear about how to follow up after the meeting. Assumptions don't work. They often lead to confusion and uncertainty, so beware of when those little buggers pop up. Instead, ask the real question.

So, what's the real question? In Brad's case, it's "Would you like to be my manager?" Or at least, "What's the next step for us?" By asking the real question, you'll get a real answer and the next steps will be clear to you. If you have an agent who's not getting you auditions, don't call them and ask how things are going. They might tell you that they celebrated their son's birthday over the weekend, which was a lot of fun, so all in all things are going really well. You asked, they answered. What can you expect? If you want to know why you aren't getting calls, ask them. Perhaps you could say, "When do you expect that I might start auditioning?" "What steps do I need to take to get some auditions?" or "So, how do you think things are going with my career?"

If you sent your headshot and demo reel to a producer you met, don't ask them if they got it. Don't even ask them if they watched it. They might answer yes to both questions, and then what? Sure, you want to confirm that they received your package and that they had a chance to watch it, but those are not the real questions. Here, the real question might be, "Can you give me feedback on my materials?" Or "Do you have a project I might be right for?"

Ask the real question. Not for their sake, but for yours. Ask the real question and get the real answer. The real answer provides real information to help you move forward. Sure by asking the real question, you risk rejection, but at least then you'll know that you've been rejected and you can move on. Asking the easy or safe questions just leaves you in limbo. Don't assume or beat around the proverbial bush. It doesn't work and it makes you feel kinda crazy.

Back to our friend, Brad. He decided to call this manager and ask her the real question. It went something like this:

BRAD:	Hi Jane. Thanks again for the meeting last week. I really connected to what you said about marketing. I'm already using the advice you gave me.
MANAGER:	Great, Brad. I enjoyed the meeting as well. What can I do for you?
BRAD:	Jane, I am calling to find out if you'd like to represent me.
MANAGER:	Well Brad, I usually call actors back for a second meeting prior to signing them. You are on my short list and I plan on making my decision at the end of the month.
BRAD:	Thanks. If I don't hear from you in the next few weeks then, may I call to follow up?
MANAGER:	Sure, but I imagine you'll hear from me soon.
BRAD:	I hope so, but if not, I'll call you on July 1st. Thanks again for the meeting, and I look forward to speaking again soon.

This story has a great ending. After asking the real question, Brad knew exactly how he would follow up with this manager. He sent her a thank you card and marked his calendar to give her a call on July 1st. She beat him to the punch, though, and called him in for a second meeting where they agreed to work together.

Brad's manager would have called him regardless of whether or not he asked the real question, but Brad didn't know that. By being clear and asking the real question, he armed himself with real information that allowed him to follow up appropriately. The real question kept him from playing the guessing game and wondering about what to do next.

How to Take a Meeting

Asking the real question really helps when it comes to agent and manager meetings, but there's more to it than that. Here are seven key points to remember when you meet with your prospective representation.

1. Do your research. Set yourself up for success by knowing the facts about whom you are meeting. Get a feel for the clients they represent, their experience in the business, and their general reputation in town. Ask around. Though the Internet has great information, the best insight you'll find comes from the people who may know them or have worked with them.

2. Be clear about your purpose. Know going in, what you want to get out of the meeting. You may just want practice taking meetings, you may want to walk out with a contract, or you may want to test the water. Know what you want so you can do your best to get it.

3. Remember that you were invited. Agents and managers are busy people. They aren't calling you in just for kicks. They are actually interested in you. Believe it or not, they invited you in because they're open to representing you. Feel confident and present yourself as a real person as well as a good actor. You don't have to show off. Just settle in and allow the conversation to flow naturally.

4. Be interested and be interesting. You're meeting with someone who just might end up working with you. In other words, you are about to embark on a relationship with this person. A relationship goes both ways, so be interested in the person across the desk from you. Find out about how they work, as well as what interests or insight they have. Allow them to talk and remember to be a great listener. Be open to sharing your personal experiences as well, so the two of you can truly get a feel for one another above and beyond the realm of acting.

5. Make a positive observation. Appreciate something about the conversation or the surroundings. Do they have a nice office? Did you learn something from them? Grab hold of something specific and toss it back to them. It's a great way to give a compliment and show that you're paying attention.

6. Ask the real questions. Ask the real question so you know exactly what's next and how to move forward. Don't be shy, just ask. Also, ask real questions throughout the meeting. Don't ask for the sake of asking. Ask because you want to know.

7. Have your own answers. The best way to tell if this agent or manager is a Collaborator is to know your own answers to the questions you ask. If you want to know how they might market you, be sure you know how you'd market you. When your answers are a match, it's likely that the relationship will be a fit too.

RELATIONSHIPS: WATER THE CROPS

THERE'S SO MUCH MORE TO DECLARATION THAN JUST meeting people and sharing your goals. Every relationship requires care and consideration, so the final aspect to cultivating relationships comes down to maintenance. As your seeds bloom into a thriving garden and you continue to pluck any weeds, you must water the crops consistently and persistently in order to enjoy healthy growth year after year. Here are nine simple ways you can maintain your Tao Declaration Garden.

1. Add value. Be willing to help others. Listen well. Go see your friends' shows. Show up on time and stay through the end. Send thank you cards. Remember birthdays. Offer help and support. Tell others about a great book you're reading or a fantastic restaurant you enjoyed. Participate because you want to, not because you have to. Share your ideas, resources and time. *The Tao of Show Business* involves a natural flow, so if you are unwilling to give things away, you actually block the natural flow of things. How can you expect people to help you when you don't first help others? Don't be the person who only contacts others when you need a favor. Stay in consistent communication so asking for help is no big deal, and receiving it is easy. Add value and increase the value of your day-to-day life.

2. Be authentic. Stop worrying about what casting directors or agents are looking for. They're looking for you, so just be yourself. Be authentically you, so that you will easily find your people. Be you and make everyone's job a little easier. My client, Justine, got fired from her fourth agent in about four years. Not because she couldn't act or even because her résumé was weak. Justine left the wrong impression with her agents every time she met with a new one. You see, Justine is really quirky and kinda clumsy. She's adorably neurotic and very marketable. Yet Justine figured the best way to take an agent meeting was to arrive all buttoned up and proper. That's what she did and agents got the message. They always sent her out on auditions for uptight professional types; the opposite of who Justine really is. It's no wonder she couldn't keep an agent. Justine wasn't her authentic self and therefore wasn't making the right match. As soon as she allowed herself to be her true self, she found the right agent who found the right auditions and Justine started booking like crazy. Be authentically you. Nobody else does you like you do!

3. Embrace the power of teamwork. Share your passion and talent with the people in your life and encourage them to do the same. John Paul Getty once said that he would rather have 1% of the effort of 100 men than 100% of his own effort. You do not have to take this journey on your own. You can enlist the support, feedback and resources of others to make things happen more efficiently and effectively. Force yourself to ask for help and be the first to offer it. Be willing to ask questions and open to receiving honest, constructive feedback. Connect people together. What better way to strengthen your team than to connect your people together! Think about the people you know and identify who they should know and why. Make introductions to support the Collaborators in your life and tie your separate circles together while you're at it.

4. Expect nothing. As cool as it would be to control everyone around you, that's just not the way it works. You can only control your own actions, so let go of any expectations you may have about who should do what and how things should all go. Don't keep score. Be responsible for your own needs and wants. Focus on you and do the things that inspire you or make you feel good. Take action because you want to, not because you have to. Release your need to be in charge and be open to any possibility. Surprise yourself.

5. Listen more and talk less. The best conversationalists are those people who listen more than they speak. Pay attention to what's going on. Observe others and learn from their successes as well as their mistakes. Make others feel appreciated because you listen to what they have to say. Even if you've heard it all before, always bring new ears and eyes to every situation in order to learn. That's how you get better.

6. Follow up and follow through. Stay in touch. Don't leave things unfinished and be mindful enough not to over-commit. Do what you say you will and communicate openly. Be honest. Don't be flakey. Show up when you say you will. Answer your phone and return phone calls quickly. Actively participate in your career and keep your word.

7. Turn your complaints into requests. Stop moaning and make change. If your scene partner isn't pulling her weight, don't bitch. Look for creative solutions and constructive ways to create new results, encourage new behaviors, or completely change your relationship. Crying won't get you anywhere, so be a part of the solution rather than the problem. If you cannot turn your complaint into a request, you have nothing to complain about.

8. Acknowledge others. There is nothing better than true appreciation. Seize every opportunity to truly acknowledge people when they help you, set a good example, take a risk, or just act like a genius. Do more than say "Hey, thanks!" Really get in there and give acknowledgement. Start by identifying a specific action this person took. Then talk about how this action reflects the kind of person they are. Finally discuss what you gained through this act or how this person inspires you. Acknowledgement is one of the coolest things you can share with the people you care about. Try it. It'll knock your socks off! Here's an example:

> *"Hey classmate! I want to acknowledge you for the bold choices you made in your scene today. You always put yourself out there and it shows how committed you are to improving your craft. Watching you really risk it and be vulnerable inspires me to be more daring as well because I see how possible it is. Rock on!"*

9. Be cool. The only power to be had exists in the present moment. Don't worry about what happened last week, about what you forgot to do, or where you dropped the ball. Stop worrying about the future, wondering about whether or not you'll get that callback or if your agent is really working hard on your behalf. You cannot change the past and you can't predict the future, so just be cool and stay present.

Now that you know about declaration and *The Tao of Show Business*, you have an incredible opportunity to connect on a new level with the people you already know. Utilize the power of teamwork to create immeasurable momentum. By sharing your long-term vision, short-term goal, and action plan with others, you can utilize their insight and expertise in order to generate exciting results as well as avoid possible pitfalls. I have worked with countless actors who fear that by reaching out to their friends or acquaintances about career stuff, they are somehow crossing a line in the relationship. This is not real. This is just fear talking. If you are truly friends with someone, they are more likely to be offended that you don't include them in your mission than if you actually asked for some help.

Gasp! How dare you include the people who care about you in your life! Unless you are someone who just despises helping others, you are crazy to think that others will despise helping you. For those of you who actually like to help others, I suggest you allow the favor to be returned.

Step One: Make a list of all the Collaborators in your personal and professional life. Feel free to list your parents, neighbors, or other people who may seem to know nothing about acting or the entertainment industry. They just might surprise you.

Step Two: Get in touch with each Collaborator on your list and share all or some of your long-term vision, your short-term goal, and your action plan. Let them know how excited you are and how committed you are to pursuing your passion. You'll probably have to play around with this a bit before you find your own way of sharing this info that feels authentic and natural to you.

Step Three: After you've shared your inspiring news, ask for any thoughts, feedback, suggestions, or referrals your Collaborators might offer you. You could ask question like these:

"*What can you think of that I might be missing?*"
"*How do you suggest I make this happen?*"
"*Who do you know that can offer some guidance?*"
"*What do you think about my plan?*"

Step Four: Allow your Collaborators to help you. Be willing to hear their thoughts and be open to whatever they have to offer. Be open to the fact that they may not want to or be able to really help you. That's cool. This exercise is about connecting with your people on new levels more than anything else. This is your chance to really make your goals public.

Step Five: Take action based on the feedback you collected from your Collaborators. Get in touch with their referrals. Try out the workshop they recommend. Be open to everything.

Step Six: Thank them. Ask them what's new in their lives and offer support. Don't forget to let them know how your plan progresses.

DECLARE THE TAO

Refer to your *Companion Workbook* and begin compiling your Collaborator list. Set dates for your contact calls and begin reaching out.

www.taoofshowbusiness.com/workbook.php

OVERCOME YOUR INNER CRITIC

Okay, we've covered positive speaking, concrete commitments, taking meetings, and cultivating relationships, but there's one last aspect to the Tao of Declaration. It's your Shadow. You know, that long dark shape that follows you everywhere, looks a lot like you, but isn't you exactly. It's that thing that never leaves your side and you know it's there, but you can't ever touch it. It's your Shadow, and between you and me, it can be a real jerk sometimes.

Your Shadow is your constant companion and it's a sly bugger who, if you're not careful, will become your worst enemy. This Shadow often reminds you that you're never good enough, you don't know enough, you're too fat or too tall or too dumb to ever accomplish anything you want. Your Shadow tells you that you don't deserve to be happy, that other people have it easy, and that you'll never change so why bother trying. Your Shadow is also a master of subtlety. It's been with you so long that it doesn't have to yell and scream in order to get its negative and degrading message across. Instead, it speaks with a small inner voice that in a simple whisper can stop you cold, create paralyzing fear, and make you feel like a big loser. Like I said, your Shadow is a real piece of work!

Though this Shadow sure looks a lot like you and feels a lot like you, this creature is not you at all! In fact, it's just a tool you created a long time ago in order to survive disappointment, rejection, danger, and disaster. The two of you have just been hanging around together for so long that you can no longer distinguish who you are from what the Shadow represents. Your Shadow loves to be in charge. When you can't tell the difference between you and it, your Shadow wins and you have no control over your career or your life.

I first met my Shadow when I was in the third grade spelling bee. It was round one; the easy, freebie round where students could practice speaking into a microphone and feel comfortable in front of an audience. Standing in front of the entire student body, I very confidently spelled the word soap, "S-O-U-P," walked back to my seat and smiled to the adoring crowd. Mr. Smith, the principal, then informed me that I misspelled the word and instructed me to leave the stage. I proceeded to walk back up to microphone and enter into a debate with him about how I clearly knew how to spell such an easy word and that he surely had it all wrong. What, did he not hear me correctly? Was he not paying attention? The mistake was his, not mine. Within moments, I realized what I had done and ran out of the gymnasium filled with laughing kids—embarrassed and ashamed.

At the age of ten, I learned that speaking in front of groups was a horrible idea and to never be too confident, because I just might make a fool of myself. And so my Shadow was born. I created this tool and gave it a very specific job. My Shadow was to do or say whatever it needed to in order to protect me from being embarrassed like that again.

As I grew up, so did my Shadow. With every scary experience, embarrassment and disappointment, my Shadow's job grew. I learned to be careful, to be cautious, to protect my heart and my ideas. My Shadow learned about the importance of keeping me safe, so this little sucker worked really hard for many years to protect me. It insulted me; it warned me of every imaginable catastrophe that might occur if I ever tried to put myself out there. My Shadow did a bang up job of protecting me, but it also prevented me from taking bold steps toward achieving my fullest potential.

You've also got a Shadow that you created years ago to protect yourself from disappointments and rejections. Though it's not too important to identify when your Shadow first appeared, think for a moment about one or two specific experiences when your Shadow may have first showed its face. When you revisit that experience, you might find that your Shadow was created out of necessity. It's just a coping tool or defense mechanism created by and for you. When you can pinpoint where your Shadow came from and realize its true purpose, you can begin to meet this voice with a discerning ear and view yourself with a little more compassion.

It's a bit ironic that while your Shadow's job is to protect you from being hurt, all it does is reinforce those fears you may already have. It insults you and scares you about what terrible things might be in store for you. Your Shadow is forced to resort to these drastic measures because you're getting smarter and more willing to make bold moves, which is a very dangerous thing for your Shadow. Remember that you gave your Shadow a job and it will do whatever it takes to perform its duties like a pro, even if it means hurting you in the process.

Though it may not always feel like it, your Shadow is actually your friend, and when used appropriately, can really come in handy. Your Shadow's an over achiever though, which can create all sorts of problems when you attempt to reach new goals, meet new people, try new things, or stretch your boundaries and really go for it.

You see, your Shadow can't tell the difference between real danger and perceived threat. It's all the same to your Shadow. So your Shadow will "protect" you from things that might actually benefit you like working to make it as an actor. For your Shadow, calling a friend to ask for acting advice is just as dangerous as jumping out of a plane without a parachute. Everything is dangerous to your Shadow, so it will whisper warnings in the form of insults or insecurities in order to prevent you from taking action. This doesn't really work when you're trying to create the career of your dreams, now does it?

So why not just knock your Shadow out with a one, two punch? Then you won't have to deal with all that negative talk that goes on inside your head, right? Then you'd be free to take risks, work hard, and finally get somewhere, right? Wrong. Your Shadow is not actually real. You can't punch it. You could try, but you'll just wear yourself out. Your Shadow actually serves a valuable purpose. You created this tool to help you survive in a sometimes-scary world. But somewhere along the way, you took a back seat to your Shadow and lost the right to control your own journey. The real trick to dealing with your Shadow is to reclaim control and cooperate with it rather than fight it. Use your Shadow as a trusted advisor, but don't let it call the shots.

Who's Speaking Here?

Before you can regain control over your Shadow, you must be able to distinguish its voice from your own. The next time you feel stuck, scared or discouraged, thinking about all the reasons why you won't make it, you'll know your Shadow's up to its old tricks. Your Shadow's voice never reflects your highest good. It never speaks to the creative, committed, charming and gifted person you really are. Your Shadow speaks to your fears, your insecurities, and your past mistakes to keep you stuck in the same old rut, which according to your Shadow is a safer place to be than out in the world turning your dreams into reality.

Your Shadow thinks it can predict the future. It knows with absolute certainty that only horrible things will result from you making that scary phone call or crashing that audition. Your Shadow also knows what other people are thinking. It reminds you that others think you're just a user when you ask for their advice or insight.

Your Shadow hopes for the worst and prepares for disaster. It believes that any one action you take will determine the demise of your career as a whole. Your Shadow is quite the drama queen, believing in black lists, ruined reputations, and curses.

Your Shadow believes in limitation. It knows that if you believe it too, you will never reach your fullest potential, so your Shadow often reminds you that you can't do stuff, you're not good enough, you're not ready, you're unlucky, or you don't know enough yet.

Your Shadow creates anxiety by reminding you of all the shoulds, musts, and have-to-dos in your life. When you operate according to what you should do rather than what you *could* do, you lose the power to choose for yourself. That's just how your Shadow likes it!

Your Shadow thrives on guilt. It will work overtime to make you feel inadequate, selfish, afraid or guilty. It loves to hold a grudge and use your past actions against you. By focusing on the past, you have no room for the future, which according to your Shadow is the perfect place to be.

Your Shadow is a law-abiding citizen. It lives according to general rules and regulations while completely ignoring your true desires. Your Shadow never rocks the boat. It never sticks up for you and always defers to the wants of others.

Do not fall victim to your Shadow's tricks. Know that your true voice only supports and encourages you. Your highest self believes anything is possible for you and champions you as you boldly take action toward the life you desire. All those other thoughts come from your Shadow. They're not yours and you don't have to buy into them.

All in all, your Shadow is fear itself. When fear runs the show, you have no options and your Shadow knows it. Your job is to regain the power by stopping the Shadow's conversation. Once you do that, you're back in the driver's seat and you can move through any fear in order to accomplish anything.

Five Steps to Keep You Moving

Step One: Stop your Shadow's crazy talk and ask yourself, "Who's speaking here?" If the conversation does not reflect your highest good, it's just your Shadow talking.

Step Two: Let it plead its case. Remember, your Shadow is designed to protect you, so go ahead and hear what on earth might be dangerous.

Step Three: Ask yourself, "How dangerous does that really feel? How likely is that to really happen?"

Step Four: Ask yourself, "What positive possibility is more likely than this fear? What's on the other side of this fear?"

STEP FIVE: Determine which option you will choose. Will you choose the fear or will you choose the incredible opportunities on the other side of it? Either way, you are predicting what *might* happen. How about choosing the option that moves you forward rather than keeping you stuck?

Remember, you win at Shadow Boxing every time you refuse to let your Shadow stop you from taking action. The goal here is not to disprove your Shadow's theories or to destroy your Shadow all together. Instead, it's just about staying energized; movin' and groovin' toward the success that surely awaits you.

You must be willing to take risks, face your fears and grow if you're ever going to realize your Tao. If your actions are inspired and connected to your purpose, you don't ever have to wonder if your decisions are correct. You never have to doubt yourself or let your Shadow get the best of you. What's the worst that will happen if you do those things that scare you? You'll survive. You'll learn from experience and keep going. Now, go work your declaration mojo!

DECLARE THE TAO

Complete the Shadow Exercise in your *The Tao of Show Business Companion Workbook.*

www.taoofshowbusiness.com/workbook.php

Setting goals, designing action plans and talking about your career are all essential steps to generating success and fulfillment as an actor. Sooner or later you must get up, leave your house and take action to bring your desires into fruition. Enter the third step of the Tao, which is to simply take action or do. Do. That's it. Just two little letters will make or break you. Chellie Campbell, financial coach and author of *Zero to Zillionaire*, wrote about the importance of taking consistent action in her first book, *The Wealthy Spirit.*

> *Thinking positive is your first step to living rich, inside and out. But it is not enough. You have to take action to achieve your goals.*
>
> *In the nineteenth century, the merchants in London built grand, tall-masted sailing ships. It would take many months, sometimes years, to build them. Then they would hire a crew, outfit the ship, and store provisions for the long sea voyage. One fine day, the ship would weigh anchor, hoist its sails, and sail out of London harbor, on its way to visit foreign ports, and trade for gold, spices, silks and jewels. The trip would take many months-often years- with no communication lines open to speak with people back home.*
>
> *Once the ship had sailed, the merchant could do nothing more; only wait for that future day when the ship would return, sail-*

ing into London harbor laden with treasure. On that day, the merchant's fortune was made. And that's where the expression, "Waiting for my ship to come in," comes from.

Some people are going down to the dock, waiting for their ship to come in– but they haven't sent any out! If you want the fortune, your responsibility each day is to send out some ships. And you had better send out more than one, because stuff happens to ships. One runs aground just outside of the harbor while another sinks in a hurricane. Pirates commandeer a few, the whirlpool gets one, and on the next one, there's a mutiny. Then, of course, there's the one that hits the iceberg.

Once you send the ship out, it's out of your control. You are only in charge of sending it out, not when it comes in.

When you get into the habit of sending ships out on a daily basis, even if you know some ships aren't going to make it back home, you are still confident and optimistic because you know you've got a whole fleet sailing out there.

Send those ships out everyday. Then prepare to unload your treasures.

Countless possible ships exist for actors. Every time you send a headshot to an agent, you're sending out a ship. Whenever you attend a workshop or networking event, you're sending out a ship. Every time you post footage on YouTube, you're sending out a ship. Classes, workshops, interning, demo reels and postcards are all great acting ships. With so many ships, it's tough to know what to choose, where to start and how to manage it all.

Everyone in this business has a different idea of what you should do, would do, or could do in order to move your career forward. Some ships will work better for you than others, and it's your job to figure out what works best for you. I'd like to share some of my insights, secrets and tips for your marketing ships that you can easily utilize in order to stand out, be riveting, and most importantly, be remembered.

You are an artist, so it's time to use your creative strengths to create unique and effective marketing ships that represent you in a dynamic and riveting way. It's time to use your art to master your business. It's time to send out some new ships. Though you may have heard a lot of advice about what defines a "good" marketing tool, I'm here to open you up to new approaches and to encourage you to find your own recipe for ship-sending success. Check it out, and have some fun sending out your ships.

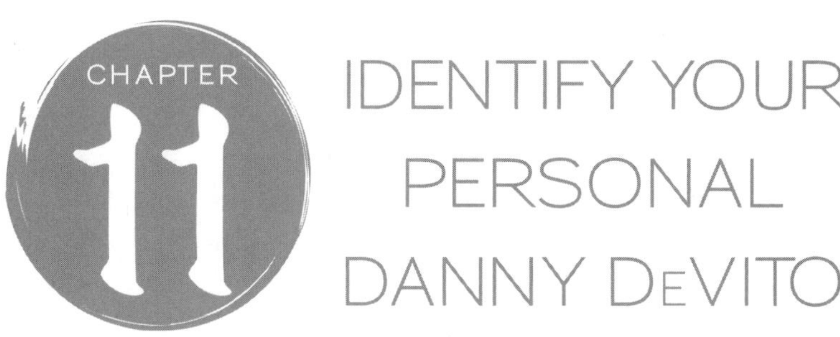

CHAPTER 11 IDENTIFY YOUR PERSONAL DANNY DEVITO

COUNTLESS SHIP SENDING OPTIONS EXIST FOR YOU. Headshots, postcards, online media, and press releases are just the tip of the iceberg. Regardless of which ships you choose, you must be certain that each marketing tool you utilize delivers a clear and consistent message. Your message should describe who you are and address how you should be cast. Your marketing tools should represent the real you and share that message with the world.

Be certain to showcase the specific qualities that set you apart from other actors in your category. What characteristics do you possess that no one else owns? Who do you know yourself to be and how do other people perceive you? When you can clearly answer these questions and relay that message in your marketing, you'll essentially eliminate your competition and carve out your own unique niche.

There's no better example of an actor who masterfully carved out his own niche than Danny DeVito. He's made quite a career for himself playing lovable yet loathsome characters. He's also a guy with certain unmistakable physical characteristics that set him apart from the crowd. He's short, bald and kinda peculiar looking. Rather than fight or hide these qualities, Mr. DeVito used them to his advantage and established himself as a Hollywood heavyweight. You see, nobody can do DeVito like he can.

Danny DeVito's story is a great one. Years ago, DeVito was appearing in an off-off-*off* Broadway show in some little hole-in-the wall theatre in New York. One night after the show, one of the top agents in the city stopped backstage to see him. He handed DeVito

his card reverently and asked him to please come see him the next day.

Danny DeVito arrived the next morning at the agent's office, located in a Manhattan penthouse with floor-to-ceiling windows overlooking the heart of Broadway. As he entered the office, the agent came around from behind his enormous desk to shake his hand.

"I just wanted to tell you that your performance last night was one of the greatest things I've ever seen in the theatre," the agent said. "And I wanted to tell you in person that I think you should get out of show business."

DeVito was disappointed to say the least. He stammered some kind of reply but didn't really know what to say.

The agent went on to explain. "You're *much* too short to make it in this business," he told him, "and your personality comes across on stage as really cocky, abrasive, and obnoxious. You'll never get work. No one would know how to cast you."

Well, Danny DeVito went home that night thinking that if someone so important in the business thought that and took the time to tell him so, he'd be a fool not to listen. So he gave up his pursuit of an acting career and went back to his previous job as a hairdresser.

But the desire to act kept bugging him. He couldn't let go. It had always been his dream, and he knew he had talent. Finally DeVito came to the conclusion that he would have to ignore the agent's sound advice, because he simply *had* to be an actor. He recognized that he was indeed extremely short and came across as really cocky, abrasive, and obnoxious, and that there was not a lot he could do about any of it. He would just have to be the best short, cocky, abrasive, obnoxious actor possible.

Short, cocky, abrasive, and obnoxious, and undeniably talented.

Danny DeVito returned to acting and, through a friend of a friend, got the chance to audition for a series regular in a new sitcom. The role didn't necessarily call for an abrasive, obnoxious actor, and it certainly didn't call for someone really, really short. At his audition, he charged into the room, climbed up on the table, threw down the script, and in his cockiest, most abrasive, most obnoxious voice demanded, "Who wrote this shit?"

He got the part. And the rest is history. Since *Taxi*, Danny DeVito has enjoyed quite a fruitful career. As of the printing of this book, DeVito has worked in over one hundred film and television projects as an actor, director or producer. Heck, he's even played Arnold Schwarzenegger's twin brother! Much of Danny DeVito's success can be attributed to his ability to embrace his own unique qualities and get specific about the types of roles he best portrays. He's done a bang-up job of clearly identifying his niche.

Queen Latifah embraced her Personal Danny DeVito when, as a successful singer and MC, she made her way onto the acting scene. She understood that industry professionals saw her as a tough, commanding, almost masculine presence and that the first roles she'd book would be tough, commanding and masculine. So rather than immediately attempting to break the mold, she embraced those qualities, did some work, and established herself as a professional. Eventually, she was able to pick and choose the kinds of projects and roles that stretched her as an actress and also stretched people's perception of her within the industry.

Today Queen Latifah is a Hollywood power player who carries her own films. She's played a sexy smoldering prison warden in *Chicago*, a meek and overworked sales clerk turned romantic adventure seeker in *Last Holiday*, and she's even a Cover Girl model... all of this because she first embraced her Personal Danny DeVito.

Charlize Theron knew that casting directors and studio executives weren't interested in looking past her external beauty when she first began her acting career. So she wisely embraced her Personal Danny DeVito and played a beautiful yet quiet female counterpart to the male lead in several films including *That Thing You Do*, *The Devil's Advocate*, and *Celebrity*.

After Theron built some credits and began creating a name for herself, she was able to move past playing just the pretty girl and began to showcase her depth and range in films like *Monster* and *North Country*. She's now an Oscar winning actress known as much for playing gritty roles as for her beauty.

Julia Roberts knows her Personal Danny DeVito. So does Tom

Hanks. John C. Reilly and Cameron Diaz do, too. Come to think of it, most successful actors today in Hollywood created long-term career success by first embracing their consistent qualities and characteristics.

These actors got super specific when they first began their careers. Doing so allowed them to more easily book work, build relationships and experience success in the industry.

You, too, have a little DeVito in you. Your Personal Danny DeVito is the perfect combination of your internal characteristics and the external impression you give others. When you can marry the two, showcase them, and apply them to the stereotypes you see in Hollywood, you will essentially eliminate your competition. Nobody can do you like you can.

I know, I know. You're an actor. You're talented and you've worked long and hard at your craft. I believe you when you say that you can play any part. But until your credits back up your chops, you must be clear and specific about your type. You must make it easy for casting directors to hire you by conveying an authentic message that showcases your character. Do not offer them a caricature of what you think they might want to see. Finally, you must be willing to risk being typecast in order to create momentum in your career.

A lot of actors fear being typecast and pigeonholed when they first begin in the business. Don't get ahead of yourself. Do what you need to do in order to begin booking jobs, and then you can worry about being typecast. Wouldn't you rather be a working actor who's making money, building relationships, and creating career momentum than someone who markets himself or herself in an unclear manner in order to avoid being typecast? Trust me. There's nothing wrong with being clear and specific. It's far better than the alternative.

The first few roles you book are often the toughest ones to snag. They're the costars, under-fives, and general one-liners that don't require much in the way of acting. More often then not, you'll book these roles based on your demeanor, your look and your relationships rather than your talent. The more specific and clear you are about your niche, the easier it'll be for casting directors and producers to hire you.

Tapping into your Personal Danny DeVito will allow you to simply embrace who you are, showcase it, and let your career unfold with ease. That's what *The Tao of Show Business* is all about.

Discovering your Personal Danny DeVito is as easy as 1-2-3

You can harness the power of your Personal Danny DeVito in three easy steps. First, you must identify the specific qualities and characteristics that you've always possessed. Think about those unique qualities you displayed as a kid that still hold true for you today. Perhaps you've always been a bit of a wild child, or maybe a little off-the-wall. Perhaps you've always been a responsible leader who people trusted to help them solve problems. Think about who you are and who you've always been, then answer the questions in the Qualities Questionnaire in your Companion Workbook. These questions will encourage you to embrace your authentic self and identify personality traits and patterns that define your Personal Danny DeVito.

DO THE TAO

Complete the Qualities Questionnaire in your *The Tao of Show Business Companion Workbook.*

www.taoofshowbusiness.com/workbook.php

Gather the Insight of Others

After you have answered your Qualities Questionnaire, it's time to gather the insight of others. You might be surprised to learn that you often give off a specific and consistent first impression upon meeting people. The truth is that casting directors assess you as soon as you walk in the door, so knowing how others initially perceive you is essential.

My client, Anne, feels like an All-American gal. She's trustworthy, cute, and somewhat conservative. Anne has always been a leader. She has a great credit score. She's responsible, sensible, and caring. Anne knows that these grounded qualities accompany her everywhere, but what she didn't know was that the first impression she leaves with people is much more controlling and Type-A. Although this realization came as a shock to her, eventually Anne used it to clarify and solidify her Personal Danny DeVito and became more accepting of how others perceive her.

Now, remember that you know yourself better than anyone, so the true value of collecting outside opinions comes when you compare that feedback to what you know to be true about yourself. It's your career; don't allow the opinions of other to dictate your actions. At the same time, receiving the input of people you trust may highlight things you forgot or tend to ignore.

You can learn more about how others perceive you with Castability Surveys. These fun questionnaires allow people who know you to apply what they know to roles you might play and qualities you display. I've included a Castability Survey in your *The Tao of Show Business Companion Workbook.* Make some copies and hand them out to your friends, co-workers, and peers. They'll be asked to identify specific roles you might play, different adjectives that describe you, as well as some of your personality traits. You'll learn a lot when you compare and contrast several people's surveys. Just look for common themes and ideas. Try it out and discover another side of your Personal Danny DeVito.

DO THE TAO

Complete the Castability Surveys in your *The Tao of Show Business Companion Workbook.*

After you have collected the feedback of at least five people you trust, it's time to compare their answers to pinpoint specific themes and embrace your Personal Danny DeVito.

www.taoofshowbusiness.com/workbook.php

Cast Yourself

The third and final step to identifying your Personal Danny DeVito is to create character descriptions that illustrate your Danny DeVito in action. Doing so will allow you to solidify on paper your essence and your specific niche. Refer to your Qualities Questionnaire and your first impression feedback from others to describe specific roles you might play.

Consider how your Personal Danny DeVito affects the characters you might play in different genres. Think about how your castability fits into independent films, television dramas, sitcoms, period pieces, and romantic comedies. What common themes show up in every character you inhabit regardless of the role itself?

Let's say your friends agree that you're refined, classy and well educated. You also know that you have a competitive streak in you. How might these qualities influence the type of dramatic roles you play? If you were cast as an attorney, what kind of attorney would you be? Would you be a successful New York corporate lawyer, climbing the ladder at your firm? Or would you play a public defender that works closely with rape victims? Would you be cunning or compassionate? Would you play by the rules or do whatever you needed to do in order to win your case? Explore and expand on how your unique essence might influence the characters you play.

What about the comedic roles you might portray? How does your Personal Danny DeVito show up in a comedy? If you were the lead in a sitcom series, what would that person be like? How might the character behave? What is unique about this character? How is this character just like you? How is it similar to other roles you've booked? Explore it and play. Then write a character breakdown illustrating who you really are.

Here are some sample character descriptions for your reading pleasure.

> ***Eric Bentley:*** *A Harvard-educated attorney. Eric comes from money, but he refuses to rely on his family's connections for personal gain. He works with an organization called The Hunger Project and is a compassionate yet fierce crusader who cares more about humanity than personal success.*
>
> ***Beth Walsh:*** *A young and simple single mom with two small kids. Recently evicted from her one-bedroom apartment, Beth finds herself returning once again to her abusive alcoholic boyfriend just to keep a roof over her children's heads. She's at a crossroads, but we know she's feisty enough to get through it.*
>
> ***Sasha Sanders:*** *The comic relief. Sasha's eccentric ideas and psychic intuitions are often too much to deal with. She's quirky to a fault and has difficulty holding down a regular job. Improv. and physical comedy a must.*

Repeat this process as often as you like. Feel free to cast yourself in a science fiction film, a gritty indie, or even Shakespeare. The more the merrier. You might even enjoy writing yourself a role on your favorite television show or film. This exercise will allow you to clarify how you're best cast and to carve out your own place in the industry.

DO THE TAO

Cast yourself and complete the Character Breakdown Worksheet in your *The Tao of Show Business Companion Workbook.*

www.taoofshowbusiness.com/workbook.php

I knew you had a little DeVito in ya! Now that you've clearly identified your Personal Danny DeVito and outlined how your unique qualities fit into the industry genres and stereotypes, you can more easily showcase your personal niche and eliminate your competition.

MASTERFUL MARKETING: HEADSHOTS

This wouldn't be a book for actors without a headshot discussion. Your headshot is the ship of all ships. It's your calling card. This 8x10 piece of paper speaks volumes for you before you ever enter a room. But not all headshots are created equal, folks, and while you are on your journey toward stardom, your headshot has a heavy load to bear.

Most actors utilize a commercial headshot along with a theatrical headshot. Here's the problem though; these photos usually feature a smiley-faced actor and a frowny-faced actor, yet neither speak to that actor's unique castability. Until your résumé stands alone, your headshot must clearly and specifically explain how you're best cast. It must represent your Personal Danny DeVito, so a handsome photo alone won't cut it. Casting directors are busy people and in order to stand out, you must convey a clear, specific message. Make their job easy. They're looking for the right actors for their projects and it's your job to showcase how right you are. Your photos must be specific.

In an effort to be specific, many actors own multiple photos featuring them in all kinds of get-ups or costumes such as a lab coat, an argyle sweater and glasses, or even a police officer's uniform. While these headshots are very specific, they don't showcase your character. They only highlight a caricature. You must, must, must avoid this at all costs. You don't need to rely on gimmicks or costumes to showcase your Personal Danny DeVito. Too often, these gimmicks just get in the way. Yeah, your shots must be specific, but they must also be authentic and believable. Casting directors may be busy, but they're not stupid. They don't need to see you wearing scrubs in order to call you in for an audition as a nurse.

You don't need a ton of specific photos with lots of specific costumes. You only need one to three key photos that speak to your castability in a drama, a comedy, and as a specific character such as a villain, a blue-collar guy, a welfare mom, or a sexy bombshell.

It *is* possible to have headshots that are both specific and authentic. Let me show you how.

Showcase the Real You

No matter what the role, you're the one being hired for the job. Your Personal Danny DeVito affects each role you book, so you've got to know yourself, know how others perceive you, and be willing to showcase your specific and authentic self. Yup, that's right. You get to be you, and the more you showcase your glorious self, the more easily success will meet you. Be your best self. Know who you are and embrace it. Do that, and you'll easily capture a riveting dramatic photo, a charming comedic photo, and perhaps an honest character shot or two.

Create a Tag Line

Now that you've outlined the types of roles you are likely to book, it's time to develop the character. Create some phrases this character would say and think the thoughts of that character during your shoot. Doing so will keep you focused on the core message of your castability so you can convey that energy through your eyes and your expression.

If you play commanding characters, you might think something like, "I'm in charge, here." If you play quirky and fun-loving comedic types, your tagline could be, "You're never going to believe this!" or "This is fun!" If you play dark brooding roles, your tagline might be, "I've got a secret," or "trust me…really."

Just develop the character enough to pinpoint possible taglines so you can convey the energy of your niche without the need for costumes, props, or gestures.

Communicate Clearly

Most actors show up to a photo shoot with just a pile of clothes and a dream. Communication with your photographer is imperative. Once you can articulate the types of roles you want to book in a way they can understand, the pressure is off. Now you can do your thing feeling confident that your photographer will work his or her magic. Illustrate your character by drawing parallels to other people. If you book sexy roles, are you Angelina Jolie-sexy or Sarah Jessica Parker-sexy? Both women are sexy, but very different. Communicate clearly enough so you know you're on the same page as your photographer. You'll be glad you did.

Less is More

Don't get too hung up on wardrobe. The perfect wardrobe is one that you don't notice. That said; make purposeful, thoughtful choices about what you wear in your shoot. Subtle hints can help illustrate who you are without slapping someone in the face with a gimmick. Once you know the message you're going for, ask yourself, "How can I convey this message in the most subtle way?"

Make the Connection

Have you ever had a conversation with someone who couldn't quite make eye contact with you? While you attempt to connect with this person, they stare at your forehead, your chest, or the top of your head. Though you continue to speak, you quickly begin to feel self-conscious or distracted by the lack of eye contact.

When choosing your headshot, make sure you can make direct eye contact with the person on the page. Print the photo out and hold it out 2-3 feet in front of you. As you look at the photo, can you lock eyes with the eyes in the headshot? Eye contact is essential to create the connection you desire with casting directors, agents, and anyone else who happens to see your headshot.

Let Go a Little

Prepare for your shoot, but then let it all go so you can actually enjoy the experience and allow your true self to shine through. You're gonna have lots and lots of headshots throughout your career. Some will work better than others, but none of them will really make or break you. You must relieve yourself (and your photographer) of the pressure around needing the perfect photo. Forget about the money you've spent. Forget about your nerves, your needs, and your time. Just enjoy the shoot. Part of an actor's job is getting your photo taken, which if you ask me is a pretty cool gig.

And Another Thing...

Remember that the sole purpose of your headshots is to get you hired. That's accomplished with a riveting photo that showcases the real you and speaks clearly to your castability. It doesn't matter if you're smiling or not. It doesn't matter if your body is off-center, or the photo is cropped tight to your head. It doesn't matter if the photo is horizontal or vertical. It doesn't matter if it's a close-up or shows a little body. What matters is that the photo captures the eye and showcases the real you. That's it.

DO THE TAO

Take a look at your current headshots and identify how you can improve them. Perhaps it's time to invest in some updated shots using your Personal Danny DeVito and the seven secrets to riveting headshots.

www.taoofshowbusiness.com/workbook.php

MASTERFUL MARKETING: POSTCARDS

I'M GUESSING THAT ALONG YOUR CAREER PURSUITS, you've encountered at least one person insisting that postcards don't work. This is simply not true. Postcard mailings can be one of the easiest ways to send out your ships. Postcards are small so they don't carry a lot of pressure. They're inexpensive, allowing you to be effective without breaking the bank. Postcards are also a fantastic way to infuse consistent energy into your career. Postcards work when you work them effectively, folks. Very practically speaking, the only way for you to become known is to stay in touch. You're more likely to be called by Clint Eastwood if he knows that you exist, so get in touch with him. Send him a postcard.

Nearly every actor I work with asks the same four questions when it comes to postcard mailings: "Who do I send them to? How often should I send them out? What the heck do I say?" and, "What should my postcards look like?" Well, here are your answers.

Your Lucky Postcard Recipients

The first step of a successful postcard campaign involves identifying your target list. I recommend splitting Your People into two groups. Group one consists of industry professionals you've met. Casting directors who've auditioned or hired you, directors or producers you've worked with, your agent, and other industry professionals you've met while networking are all Your People and honorary members of your Fan Club, which has an easy lifetime membership program.

Group two consists of industry professionals who you'd like to meet or work with. They are future Fan Club members, but for now let's put them on your Hit List. With hundreds, even thousands of potential Hit List members, I'd like to suggest a few methods to narrow this group down to a manageable number. It's important that your Hit List members be in line with your career goals, so if you want TV credits, target casting directors, producers and directors who work in television. If you'd like to establish yourself as a force in the independent film arena, target those people who actually work in independent films.

Compiling Your Television Hit List

First, research the television programs where the most opportunity exists for co-star and guest-star roles. This may or may not include your favorite shows, but it must include those programs whose plots require frequent new characters such as *Law and Order*, *CSI* or any other procedural drama. Do yourself a favor and pare this down to a manageable list so you can easily and consistently target these people. Remember that less is more when it comes to effective marketing.

Next, locate the current and updated mailing addresses for the casting directors and/or producers of your list of shows. Casting directors notoriously move from location to location, so take the time to confirm the most recent address information. Two fabulous resources for up-to-date casting addresses are www.imdbpro.com (very different from the simple www.imdb.com and worth every penny) or www.castingabout.com.

Compiling Your Film Hit List

Unlike television, film-casting director information can be trickier to find because films don't necessarily stick to an annual production routine like a lot of television. But it's still possible to send your ships out.

First, create a list of your favorite films from the previous few years and identify the directors, producers, and casting directors for each project.

Second, visit imdbpro.com and do some research. Check out what other projects these people have worked on and who else they've worked with. After digging a little deeper, you will begin to notice that producers often work with the same directors who tend to work with the same casting directors. These are the names for your film Hit List.

This strategy works when researching genres as well. If you love romantic comedies, check out recent romantic comedies online and see who cast them. If you're itching to star in a Sundance Film Festival winner, you could also check out the website for Sundance, find out the winning directors from previous years, and see what they're currently up to on www.imdbpro.com. From there, you'd identify the casting director's name for each director's current project.

When members of your Hit List are currently casting or are in production on a project, you can send your little postcard ship their way.

This strategy serves two purposes. First, it provides direction and allows you to get specific about who you are targeting. Second, it forces you to clarify and simplify your immediate career goals and marketing strategy. It also relieves you of any pressure to market to *everybody*, so you can avoid feeling overwhelmed.

Your Masterful Marketing Timeline

When you consistently target a specific group of people over the course of several months, you are well on your way to postcard mastery. After you've pinpointed your Fan Club and Hit List members, it's time to create your mailing timeline. I recommend executing a mailing every four to eight weeks. Though it may feel like overkill, it's safe to assume that not every postcard gets the attention it deserves. Therefore, a four to eight week timeline ensures that your message will be received on a semi-regular basis.

Okay, I know what you're thinking, "Every four to eight weeks!

What if I don't have anything to report?" Good point. I've heard a lot of casting directors and other industry professionals urge actors not to mail them a postcard until they have progress to share. I agree with them 100%. And if you feel like you have nothing worthy of reporting, you are most certainly not giving yourself enough credit. You're an actor. You study your craft, you audition as often as you can, you book jobs, you showcase, you learn new dialects and cultivate new relationships. You travel, workout, learn new languages, become wine connoisseurs, and learn to salsa dance. All of these diverse and impressive feats are more than update worthy. Industry professionals understand that success in this business is a journey. They just want to hear from you about your progress, which is not limited to simply booking jobs or winning awards. Your accomplishments do not have to be of biblical proportions before you share them. Give yourself a break and more importantly, give yourself some credit. You're a genius and Your People want to hear about it.

So Much to Say

Here comes the part that trips a lot of actors up: the message on the postcard. Yes, your message is important, but the real reason postcards work comes down to the frequency of your mailings as well as the specificity of your recipient lists. So take a deep breath and let go of the pressure to write the perfect message. It's not as big a deal as you think. Your postcard message can follow a simple yet thorough recipe featuring your angle, an update, and a call for action. Let me walk you through it.

Part One: Angle

First comes your angle, which basically just describes you in a nutshell. A few years ago, I listened to a panel of A-List publicists speak about how they operate in the industry. I had the opportunity to ask them about what criteria an actor must meet in order to utilize their services. Each publicist agreed that (fees aside) they'd work with any actor who has an angle they can believe in.

So what's an angle? An actor's angle speaks to their unique niche, or Personal Danny DeVito. It sets them apart by showcasing who they are and how they're different from other actors out there. Your angle can be written similarly to a newspaper headline and must be colorful and captivating, enticing it's reader to continue on.

Creating your angle is easy breezy. Begin by selecting two diverse and dynamic adjectives that vividly describe your essence and range as an actor. Trust me, it's a lot easier to come up with colorful adjectives when you take yourself out of the equation.

In order to capture truly riveting descriptions, I recommend that you draw character parallels to actors you relate to. Turn to the Character Parallels Worksheet in your handy workbook. There, list at least ten actors whose performances resonate with you. Describe each actor with one or two colorful adjectives. Please avoid just listing actors who look like you and try to pick diverse performers of different genres, ethnicities, age ranges, and sex. When you do, your adjectives will become unique and diverse. Your character parallel list may look something like this:

Denzel Washington	*commanding*
Cate Blanchett	*fearless*
Christopher Walken	*fierce*
Allison Janney	*savvy & smart*
Katharine Hepburn	*independent*
Harrison Ford	*subtle*
Johnny Depp	*one-of-a-kind*
Edward Norton	*surprising*

Now take a look at your dynamic list of adjectives. You'll notice that those words also describe who you are and what you bring to the characters you play. Just like that, you have a diverse and colorful list of adjectives you can use to describe yourself in your angle. Pretty cool, huh?

After you have selected a couple of unique adjectives from your list, it's time to round out your angle. Pair two adjectives with your favorite element of acting, a description of the roles you play, or a specific talent you possess. Feel free to cut out any extra words and punctuation here and to be as concise as possible. Check out these example angles:

Savvy and Smart Leading Lady
Fearless and Surprising Everyman
One-of-a-Kind Comedic Genius
Commanding and Fearless Scene Stealer
Fierce Yet Subtle Callback King

Part Two: Update

After you have created a few angles that jive for you, it's time to add your update. This second portion of your postcard text simply answers the question, "What's up lately?"

Take a moment to brainstorm every step you've taken in your career over the past three months. Write these wins down and use them as updates. Don't judge yourself or your accomplishments. They all count. Go ahead and write them all down. Possible updates include:

Went to producers for Grey's Anatomy.
Just wrapped the indie film, Clover's Big Adventure.
Performing improv. Friday night at Laugh City.
Currently rocking my scene study class with Nancy Ferguson.
Just booked national Kia *commercial.*

Try keeping an update log throughout the month where you can jot down small wins, successes or active steps you've taken for your career. You can review your log each month or so when you sit to compile your postcards. Instead of racking your brain to think of an appropriate career update, you'll now have a long list of wins to choose from. Remember that industry pros just want to see your progress. Keep your update relevant to your career, but don't judge yourself if you feel like you have nothing to say. Get creative and give yourself some credit.

Part Three: Action

Now, it's time to specify your intention behind your postcard with a call for action. Though it may seem obvious to you what your intention might be, (duh… you're an actor sending a postcard to an agent) you cannot assume that the postcard's recipient gets it. *The Tao of Show Business* is all about energy, so by specifically stating what you want, you are energetically sending a powerful message that you're ready and willing for the next step. Get specific with your call for action.

Here come the examples:

Seeking new representation. Let's meet!
I'd love to audition for your film.
Please come see my show this weekend.
I look forward to meeting you at next week's casting workshop.
Thanks for the great class. I'd love to audition for you.

Again, I urge you to keep an ongoing list of possible angles and updates. Doing so will make managing your monthly postcard mailings a snap because you'll have tons of colorful slogans to choose from. Below are some completed postcard scripts featuring angle, update, and action. Enjoy!

Savvy and Smart Leading Lady
Went to producers for Grey's Anatomy.
Seeking new representation. Let's meet!

Fearless and Surprising Everyman
Just wrapped the indie film, Clover's Big Adventure.
I'd love to audition for your film.

One-of-a-Kind Comedic Genius
Performing improv Friday night at Laugh City.
Please come see my show this weekend.

Commanding and Fearless Scene Stealer
Currently rocking my scene study class with Nancy Ferguson.
I look forward to meeting you at next week's casting workshop.

Fierce yet Subtle Callback King
Just booked national Kia *commercial.*
Thanks for the great class. I'd love to audition for you.

Designing Your Postcards

Now that you know whom to target, when to mail your postcards, and what to say, you get to use your creativity and play with your postcard design. Though your postcards can look any way you like, you must include your name and contact information so people can actually get in touch with you. If you have trepidation about publishing your phone number and email address on a card that'll just be floating out there for any perverted postal worker to snatch, you're not alone. Unfortunately though, you must publish contact information in order for your postcards to generate results. To maintain your privacy, consider using a message service or a specific email address just for acting so you can exercise caution. If you have an agent, list their phone number. But always include yours as well. Many times, casting directors will hang on to your postcard for months, even years. By the time they actually call you, your agent might be long gone. Always include your direct contact information in all of your marketing materials.

Outside of including contact information on your postcard, anything goes design-wise. Most postcards are just a 4x6 version of an actor's headshot. That works, but you can also be creative and use your postcard design to illustrate your Personal Danny DeVito. I've had actors print everything from a cartoon drawing of their headshot, a photo of a group of Elvis impersonators grocery shopping, to still photos from a movie set on their postcards. Some actors hire graphic designers or artists to create a unique postcard design that represents the actor's brand. Even other actors turn their favorite snapshots of pets, trips, or special events into postcards. When it comes to design, anything goes. Have some fun. You're an artist for Pete's sake, so be artistic and creative.

Now, remember that it's about consistency and persistence with your postcard mailings. If you're avoiding a mailing until you're struck with a divine idea for the perfect postcard, let it go. Those little ships can't do their jobs sitting on a shelf somewhere. Print up a simple headshot version of your postcard and get things moving. The toughest part about finishing a postcard mailing is starting it. Don't wait. Just begin and trust that new ideas will come to you the more frequently you practice this postcarding thing.

Play With Your Postcard Packaging

On a final note about postcards, let's address some small tricks and tips to increase your chances for success.

1. Place your postcard in an envelope, and not just any envelope. Visit a stationery or paper supply store to discover an envelope that represents your unique essence. Ask yourself, "If I were an envelope, what would I look like?" Mailing your postcard in a fancy envelope sets your card apart from the pack. Recipients may even think it's an invitation or a check, which they'll be eager to open.

   A client of mine recently did a postcard mailing to talent managers. She designed a pretty basic card, but mailed them all in lovely metallic envelopes. One manager was lucky enough to receive his postcard on his birthday and immediately opened it. He then called my client, told her how she had fooled him, then thanked her for the mailing and invited her in for a meeting.

2. Personalize your stamps. You gotta love technology! Today you can customize your postage stamps at www.stamps.com, www.zazzle.com, or www.photostamps.com. What a fun way to include your photo on a unique envelope.

3. Experiment with different layouts and sizes. It's not necessary to always use the same photo or design with every postcard mailing. That's a surefire way to lose steam in your marketing if you ask me. As long as each postcard represents your Personal Danny DeVito, you can mix it up as often as you like.

DO THE TAO

Put these tips into action and complete a postcard mailing to your Fan Club and Hit List within the next fifteen days.

www.taoofshowbusiness.com/workbook.php

GENERATE SOME BUZZ

What if I told you that you are only days away from reading press about yourself in various national publications ranging from the *Hollywood Reporter* and *Variety* to the *Los Angeles Times* or *New York Times*? It's true. With just a little work, you can easily generate press and media buzz about your career regardless of how famous you may be. Celebrities, top corporations, non-profit organizations and politicians rely on publicists to create public awareness and media buzz. It's a publicist's job to present newsworthy information about their clients on a consistent basis in order to maintain momentum for their clients' careers. Well, until you have your very own publicist, you can easily do the job of generating buzz by writing and publishing press releases.

Simply put, a press release is a newsworthy statement specifically prepared for media distribution. A press release provides journalists with publication-ready information that's useful, accurate and interesting. Journalists are very busy people, always looking for good story, and press releases actually make their jobs easier. When a reporter receives a press release that's interesting, relevant to potential readers, well written and ready to go, that lucky little reporter has a lot less legwork to do. They can simply print that release or use it to springboard further research for a new story about the same topic.

How to Write a Press Release

The trick to writing a press release is to think like a reporter. You must convey information about yourself with an interesting angle and make the release intriguing and relevant. If you think you don't have anything newsworthy to report, it's important to give yourself a break here. Give yourself the credit you deserve and take an objective look at the progress you've made, the projects you're working on, and the value you add to the business as a whole. Just put your publicist's hat on and make it work.

I recently helped a client named Janine craft a press release. Janine was convinced that writing an intriguing release would be impossible. Returning to acting after a four-year hiatus, she had no recognizable credits, no agent, and no union membership. Janine also feared that industry pros might judge her as not being far enough along for her age.

So we decided to write a press release that played to the giant pink elephant in Janine's mind. We wrote about how, at forty-one, she is finally taking her career into her own hands by producing her own material. In the release, Janine even talks about how valuable her hiatus was and how it now allows her to pursue her career with excitement as well as balance. The release was not only intriguing, but also extremely honest. This level of honesty immediately eliminated the self-judgment Janine was feeling, which really freed her up to market herself more openly.

You are creative, proactive, smart, savvy and busy. So write about it. Before you can craft a press release, you must decide on the approach or topic of your release. Take ten minutes to write down everything you've accomplished over the past twelve months - personally and professionally. Take a look at your list and identify any themes or through-lines.

Your list might look something like this:

- *Shot a webisode series*
- *Created Facebook account*
- *Promoted to advanced level in acting class*
- *Wrote first draft of screenplay*
- *Formed an Improv. Troupe*
- *Improv. Troupe won five contests*
- *Began blogging every week*
- *Got a dozen commercial callbacks*
- *Auditioned for co-star on NBC series*

One possible theme in this list is the online presence you've created by blogging, and Facebooking your heart out. You could write a press release about the momentum you are building through the Internet. Voila! Just like that… a newsworthy, relevant angle featuring little ol' you! Take your ego or inner critic out of it and do your best to deliver a sharp story angle that will be of real interest to the public.

Once you've identified your topic, you can then turn your attention toward crafting a snazzy press release. Press releases have a specific format you must follow to set yourself up for success. Here it is:

At the top-left side of your press release, feature your contact information including your phone number and email address. To the right of the contact information, type "For Immediate Release" in capital letters. This means that your article is ready to go without any specific time constraints.

Next comes your headline, which is featured in all capital letters across the top of the body of your press release. Grab the most newsworthy idea or angle and state your headline in as few words as possible. I recommend that you emulate the headlines featured in the news publications you hope to be featured in.

Don't forget about the subhead, which gives you the opportunity to expand on your topic without stepping on the drama of the press release headline.

With your topic identified and your headline intact, it's time to compose the body of your press release. Here's a quick crash-course in journalism: the first 100 words or so must be riveting enough to capture the reader's attention and entice them to read on. Often called the lead, it's the most important aspect to a successful press release. Your lead must address the *who, what, when, where* and *how* of the story.

The rest of your press release serves to support and expand on whatever claims were made in the lead and headline. You can site resources or quote yourself as though you've been interviewed. Just remember to be succinct, keep it interesting and factual. Remember that shorter is better, so do your best to limit the release to one page.

End your press release with what journalists call the boilerplate. The boilerplate essentially summarizes biographical information about you that can be used repeatedly in future articles.

Conclude your press release with ###. This signifies the end of the document to the reporters who'll be receiving your release.

If you really want to tackle this press release writing thing, check out the following websites for even more information: www.publicityinsider.com, www.prweb.com, and www.press-release-writing.com.

Here's a sample press release for your reading pleasure:

Contact: Jack Smith
Tel: (310) 555-5555
Cell: (310) 444-4444
Email: jacksmith@email.com

FOR IMMEDIATE RELEASE

NEW TALENT CATAPULTS CAREER WITH NEW MEDIA
Jack Smith Generates Industry Buzz Online

Los Angeles, June 18, 2008 – In just two short years, Jack Smith has taken himself from an unknown comic to an internationally recognized face thanks to new media. Virtually unknown by Hollywood insiders, Jack Smith launched his career with his online series, *Comic Pizza*. This weekly series features Smith and friends in candid, provocative, sometimes crass comedy sketches. Last week alone, *Pizza* boasted online views well into the six figures.

Jack Smith is not alone. In 2006, Time Magazine highlighted the rise in the sharing of online content and the importance of the emerging online community. Now, filmmakers clamor to capitalize on this global audience.

Earlier this year, Joss Whedon launched *Dr. Horrible*, starring *How I Met Your Mother's* Neil Patrick Harris. *Horrible* is the first webisode series to successfully generate revenues through viewer downloads. Smith joins Whedon, and a host of other producers who have their eyes on the Internet horizon.

"The Internet is where it's at. I just feel lucky that I recognized it long before the Hollywood machine," says Smith. "I decided to stop waiting to be hired and finally start working."

Thanks to new media outlets such as YouTube.com and FunnyOrDie.com, actors just like Smith are generating their own work and finding an audience online.

Jack Smith knows where the entertainment industry is headed and he's taking advantage of it. He says, "New media is the future of this industry. The fact that I can write, produce, and distribute impressive and intelligent material puts me ahead of the game and in charge of my career."

For more information, visit www.JackSmith.com or www.comicpizza.com

###

Okay, It's Written... Now What?

It may seem unlikely, but you'll be surprised by how easy it is to do what media pros call "getting ink". All you need to do is get your completed press release into the hands of publications such as *Variety*, *The Hollywood Reporter*, *Entertainment Weekly*, and even *Backstage*. These media outlets will then transform your press release into real-life news by it or publishing it in their online editions.

Let's say you want to see your name in the *Daily Variety*. First, you've got to find out who the appropriate editor or writer might be. I'd start by visiting *Variety*'s website to find the name and phone number or email address for the editor or perhaps a specific department of the magazine. Next you can simply email or fax your mighty press release off to that person. Ta-dah! It's that easy. Really.

Do this repeatedly for every publication you wish to contact. Sometimes you may find that no contact information is listed on the media outlet's website. If that's the case, try giving them a call to ask for the editor's name and fax number. Though not every magazine will choose to run your story, if you do this consistently enough, you're bound to get some ink sooner or later.

Getting your press release out to a broad audience is now even easier than emailing it out to one publication at a time. You can hire a service such as www.ereleases.com or www.spotlightprcompany.com to submit your release on your behalf. It'll cost you a couple hundred bucks, but the time and guesswork it saves is priceless.

Set Yourself Up for Success

Your press release is gonna get snatched up and reproduced out in the world, so it's essential that you create a system that allows you to track your media blurbs and use them to your advantage. You can do this by creating a Google Alert that notifies you whenever your name shows up in cyberspace. Just visit www.google.com/alerts and ask Mr. Google to notify you whenever your name is published online. Google will then email you links to articles and media blurbs featuring none other than you. Pretty cool, huh?

As you begin to receive alerts from Google, you can use this press to create one-sheets, media kits, and other marketing materials. For example, you could include quotes from different publications on your website. You could print a blurb from *Variety* on your postcards. Or you could create an entire one-sheet featuring different articles, stories, or references to the ever-talented-and-talked-about-you. The more ink you collect, the more you have to offer when you take agent or producer meetings. Now you've got evidence of all the newsworthy work you're up to!

Keep the Ball Rolling!

Joseph, a client of mine, executed a brilliant press release that generated some pretty decent buzz. But even better than the original press release were his diligent follow-up efforts. Joseph set up his Google Alert and collected media as it began popping up online. He then forwarded these articles to his Hit List and Fan Club expressing excitement and curiosity about how to take advantage of his media momentum. Simply by sharing the news with His People, Joseph began getting great support and suggestions that quickly turned into meetings and movie offers. He went from being an unknown actor to a rising star with multiple movie deals all thanks to the press buzz he created for himself and the thorough follow-up he executed.

Joseph understood the job of a publicist and decided to become his own publicist in order to get the ball rolling in his career. You can do it too! Just start by writing a great release, set yourself up for easy follow up and then share the good word with Your People.

DO THE TAO:

Compose your press release and use this follow-up system to generate some buzz and create some career momentum.

www.taoofshowbusiness.com/workbook.php

Chapter 15: Masterful Marketing: Cover Letters and One-Sheets

WRITING THE IDEAL COVER LETTER CAN BE CHALLENGING. How on earth are you supposed to express your true essence on a sheet of paper? Besides, most agents and other bigwigs don't even read cover letters, right? Wrong! If you write a cover letter expecting no one to read it, you'll write a letter unworthy of being read. If, on the other hand, you utilize The Four Fundamentals format and really write that thing, you just might find that your letter gets read. Your cover letter doesn't need to say everything; it just needs to express The Four Fundamentals in a concise and engaging way.

Part One: Connection

The first thing your letter must do is establish a connection between you and its reader. Connection speaks to who you are, who they are and how you relate to one another. Illustrate how you know the person you are writing and define the relationship.

Referrals really work, so use 'em when you've got 'em. Talent agent and author of *An Agent Tells All*, Tony Martinez, explains the importance of utilizing industry referrals. He writes, "I never, ever ignore referrals. If someone in the business asks me to meet an actor, I'll do it. It's a matter of respect." If you have a referral or recommendation, begin your letter with that. Establish a connection with your reader right off the bat.

Don't panic. If you do not have a referral to whomever you are writing, simply establish a similar connection in order to encourage your reader to take a meeting with you. The connection can be strong regardless of how "connected" you feel. You've selected this person for a specific reason, so outline what that reason is. Establish your own connection. Try these on for size:

> *My name is Jane Actor and your client,*
> *Joe Director, referred me.*
>
> *I recently graduated from your alma mater, USC.*
>
> *I'm currently seeking new representation,*
> *and you are at the top of my list.*

Part Two: Commitment

Be sure to outline what you stand for. Show the reader your dedication, your progress, and your commitment to your career. Plant yourself firmly in your commitment to acting and really express your vision, goals, or desires. When you engage the reader and illustrate that you are more than what can be expressed on the page, you know your cover letter is on the right track. Check out commitment in action:

> *Your refusal to sacrifice your vision for the sake of the box office illustrates the level of integrity I strive for daily. That's why I'd be honored to meet with you to discuss our careers.*
>
> *I am an endearing comedic actor committed to booking a*
> *comedy pilot this season. After two years of intense training*
> *and expanding my résumé with four television credits,*
> *I am confident that this is my year of the series regular.*
>
> *I'm an animal lover and world traveler. My compassion*
> *for others motivates me to volunteer my time at*
> *The Women's Center. I always bring that same*
> *compassion to the roles I play.*

Part Three: Angle

Sound familiar? Your angle addresses the "why." Now it's time to share what you have to offer. What sets you apart from other actors? Your angle can be concise, but it must be eye-catching. Now it's time to brag. Talk about your recent successes, bookings, or celebrations. Don't be shy.

> *My love of cooking exotic meals illustrates my sense of adventure. This same fearlessness motivates my choices while acting.*

> *I just completed Elizabeth Allen's Master Intensive.*

> *I've booked seven of the last eight*
> *commercials I've auditioned for.*

Part Four: Action

Your call for action clearly outlines the next step. What do you want your reader to do? What action do you plan to take? Try to keep the ball in your court by making the follow-up your job rather than your reader's. Action explains the specific purpose of your letter and sets up the expectation for what's next. For example:

> *I am currently taking meetings with prospective agents and will call your office next Thursday to discuss working together.*

> *I understand that this is your show's final season, and kindly ask for the opportunity to audition before the show wraps.*

> *I've been looking forward to meeting you in person and will be sure to introduce myself at your workshop next week.*

By applying The Four Fundamentals to your cover letters you'll present a clear, concise and intriguing message and set yourself up for easy follow through. Here's an example of a completed cover letter a client of mine used in her effort to land an agent:

Dear Mr. Agent Person,

My acting coach, Joe Director referred me. I am committed to furthering my television career and need strong representation in order to do so.

Given my commitment, I study diligently with Joe and workshop regularly in order to build relationships. I consider myself to be a life long learner who always works to improve my craft, my knowledge, and my skills in all areas of life.

The passion I feel for life and learning permeates every aspect of my acting career. Acting has carried me from Seattle to London to New York and beyond.

After graduating with honors from the University of Southern California, I starred in Sally Kendall's award winning independent film, *Daisies Everywhere* as well as the long-running play, *Forget Me Not* here in Los Angeles. I am proud of the success I've had and the relationships I've built with industry professionals such as Sean Stevens, Harry Harper, and Janet Jones.

I am looking to you for your experience, your relationships, your expertise, and your initiative. Joe sings your praises and I admire the strong reputation you have built throughout your 12 years in the entertainment industry. I know we could build a solid partnership together and kindly ask for the opportunity to meet.

I respect your time and know that you are incredibly busy, but I would love to discuss working together. I will follow up with a phone call next Tuesday to set up a meeting.

Very Sincerely,

Jane Actor

DO THE TAO

Use The Four Fundamentals to craft a cover letter you can be proud of. Refer to the worksheet in your *The Tao of Show Business Companion Workbook.*

www.taoofshowbusiness.com/workbook.php

What's a One-Sheet?

Sometimes, you may find that it's easier to speak about yourself in third person rather than pour your heart out in a cover letter. A one-sheet acts as your advertisement showcasing The Four Fundamentals from an objective third party rather than little ol' you.

A one-sheet might feature character descriptions of roles you play, rave reviews from magazines, your biography, recent career updates and successes, or even photos. Simply put, a one-sheet is another way to showcase your glorious self in a creative way outside of the same old boring cover letter. Here's a sample one-sheet to illustrate my point:

Stop Looking! You've found her…
LOVABLE AND FIERCE, TALENTED AND PROFESSIONAL

Jane Actor

Jane's time competing in the Miss Washington Scholarship pageant helped her pay for her B.F.A. in Acting from Washington State University. She then traveled throughout Europe and studied acting in London. Upon her return to the US, Jane spent time touring and performing in cities such as New York and Chicago, and Washington DC. After enjoying critical acclaim for her one-woman show, *Jane's Show*, Jane landed in Los Angeles, where she works as an actor in film and TV.

RECENT SUCCESSES:

- Booked *Dunkin' Donuts Commercial*
- Starring in hilarious web-series "Can't You Tell?"
- Perfecting her craft at Sue Ponto's Actor Training
- Tracy Blakely advanced commercial class graduate.

RAVE REVIEWS:

"Actor shines onstage and effortlessly delivers a stunning, yet human performance." —**Stage Magazine**

"Jane Actor's forceful and commanding portrayal of Suzanne is the work of a moving star in the making. Watch out for this fine performer."—**Jon Ashton,** ***Weekly News***

Seeking New Representation
555.123.4525 / janeactor@yahoo.com

DO THE TAO

Combine your biography, headshots, character descriptions, career highlights, or rave reviews with creative formatting, colors and design to create your very own one-sheet.

www.taoofshowbusiness.com/workbook.php

MASTERFUL MARKETING: DEMO REELS AND THE WEB

An actor without a demo reel is a person with a fun hobby. A demo reel is one tool that separates the professional actor from someone who is just trying to do the acting thing. Don't be that person. Get yourself a demo reel you can be proud of.

Let me guess... you're waiting for footage from a project you shot nine months ago. Perhaps the footage you do have from that indie you did last year has horrible sound quality, so you can't use it. Well, you do not have to wait around for footage to appear before you create your demo reel.

Contrary to what you might think, you are completely in charge of whether or not you have a reel and whether or not it's a tool you that makes you proud. *The Tao of Show Business* is all about consciously flowing through your career feeling empowered, proactive and balanced rather than waiting, resisting or putting your life in the hands of others.

Your demo reel's purpose is to showcase your chemistry with the camera, highlight your acting chops, and display your range and Personal Danny DeVito. Rather than summarize the work you've done in the past, your reel provides the opportunity to reflect where you want to take your career. Don't fall into the thought-trap that you must wait for real (whatever the heck that word means) credits before you put your reel together. That belief doesn't serve you and it's just not true. Let go of your need for the perfect reel and set yourself up for success by having a reel right now. I wish I had a dollar for every actor I know who didn't have a reel they loved, met an industry professional who asked to see their work on tape, and then scrabbled around the city for a week slapping some footage together.

Owning a fantastic demo reel is as simple as you'd like it to be. Today, most demo reels are between 60 and 90 seconds; just long enough to showcase your talent without boring the viewer to tears. Keep in mind that your reel's job is to showcase your acting. Acting is something you can do, so pick a scene or two you like, rehearse with a fellow actor and shoot the darn thing already! Don't worry about props or crazy lighting tricks, just showcase the talented genius you are with a script that speaks to you.

I bet you even know some friends with all the equipment you might need for your shoot. Do your best to get a decent camera, ensure the lighting is right, and the sound is audible and clear. Keep the production level super simple so it doesn't distract from the purpose of your reel – your acting chops.

If you can't get your hands on a good camera, you can also check out services such as www.speedreels.com or www.reelaccess.com. Both companies will shoot your project for you, and it won't cost you an arm and a leg.

Some actors make the mistake of distracting from their talent by including music montages, headshot slideshows, or lengthy scenes focusing too much on the other actors. Keep it simple. Don't distract your viewer with these superfluous extras.

Once your demo reel is complete, it's time to show it to people. You can save yourself a lot of time and money by simply hosting your demo reel online rather than reproducing a bunch of hard copies. Don't forget to add it to your Actor's Access account while you're at it. Did you know that attaching media to your online submissions greatly increases your chances of securing auditions? Actor's Access moves actors with reels to the front of their casting submission lines, making a reel even more valuable.

Though I've expressed some urgency here about the importance of owning a demo reel, please continue to proactively market yourself while you are getting your reel together. Yes, it's important. But more important is your need to maintain momentum in your career. Put that reel on your to-do list and begin taking action toward it, but don't abandon all your other ships while you work on your reel.

DO THE TAO

Create your demo reel plan in your *The Tao of Show Business Companion Workbook.*

www.taoofshowbusiness.com/workbook

Put Yourself on Tape

A lot of actors express frustration about not having access to their dream auditions. They say that if only they could "get in the room" they'd be able to book the job. The toughest part about booking a job is just getting in the room. Well, perhaps you don't have to wait to find an agent who can hopefully get you into the big audition rooms. Maybe you can instead film an audition for that dream role and submit your DVD to the producer, casting director, or director of the film.

Did you know that Vera Farmiga landed the role of Madelyn in Martin Scorsese's film, *The Departed* because she created an audition tape and sent it directly to Mr. Scorsese?

Imagine if you directed the same amount of energy toward creating audition tapes that you do toward finding an agent, mailing your headshots, or complaining that you just can't seem to get in the room. Take your career into your own hands and shoot your own audition. Put yourself out there in a big way and watch what big results just might come of it. You have nothing to lose.

Create Your Online Presence

I could fill this entire book with success story after success story of actors I've worked with that have created their own big break by sending their ships out into cyberspace. Can you think of a larger ocean than that?

You do not have to wait around to be hired in order to act in great projects that generate buzz for you. You can star in your dream projects today if you want to. It just involves some creativity, teamwork, and some cyber-ship sending. Thanks again to YouTube and the like, you can create a webisode series online and truly take your career into your own hands. Creating a webisode series is easier than you think.

STEP ONE: Create a story idea. Plan it out on paper and try to create a story arc that has legs for multiple webisodes. If writing is not your cup of tea, feel free to utilize the skills of your creative friends with a passion for the pen.

STEP TWO: Do some research to see what else is out there. Be sure to watch some other webisode series to identify what works and what you'd improve.

STEP THREE: Write the script. Again, don't be shy about asking your talented and wonderful friends to participate with you in creating this series. You don't have to do it alone.

STEP FOUR: Compile your team. Bring in the actors and necessary crew to make the shoot run as seamlessly as possible. Call in favors from those people you've done free work for in the past.

STEP FIVE:	Download the film from your camcorder to your computer. Edit the film with the film editing software that probably came with your computer. Now add titles, opening and closing credits and any other special effects you want.
STEP SIX:	Upload the webisode to your own website. Or, upload it to other traffic-heavy sites like YouTube.

Did you know that most major talent agencies, studios, and networks hire people to surf the Internet in order to discover what people out there in cyberspace are watching?

My client, Janet, created a two-woman comedy show with her friend. They performed the show at a few theatres around Los Angeles and then put it up on YouTube. Within weeks, their show created significant industry buzz thanks to the Internet audience they had attracted. Janet and company soon began getting development meetings and their live show performed to sell-out crowds. A few months later, they were even flown to Paris and awarded first prize at a local film festival. All because they stopped waiting to be hired, created good work and hosted it on the Internet.

Don't wait for opportunities to knock on your door! Go out there and do what you're good at: act! Showcase your creativity online and soon enough, you'll be thanking YouTube in your Oscar speech!

Outside of posting your work online and creating your own audition DVDs, I also recommend that you create a strong Internet presence. Make sure information about you and your acting is readily available on websites such as imdbpro.com, Facebook, and even your own site. Don't forget that this information is available for all to see and people are looking, so be smart and present yourself professionally in cyberspace. I had a client actually lose an acting job after the producers of the show found her Myspace page. Your career unfolds a little more each and every day, so treat it with the respect it deserves.

CHAPTER 17 THE MOTHER OF ALL SHIPS

THE MARKETING IDEAS PRESENTED IN THIS BOOK are pretty incredible if I do say so myself. But let me be very clear—the best way to move your career forward is to open your mouth and ask your friends, classmates, relatives, and acquaintances for help.

No headshot, postcard, or fancy press release you send out can measure up to the effectiveness of the relationships you cultivate. So, have fun sending out your ships, but don't forget to utilize the mother of all ships—your ability to enlist the help and support of other people. Pick up the phone, send an email, and reach out on a consistent basis. It's the best way to master the Tao and take your career to new heights.

My client, Stephanie, and I worked for about six months on her marketing strategy. Stephanie wanted to land an agent, so we developed her Hit List, we got her some great headshots, we crafted a cover letter, we did everything. And we got her a handful of meetings. The meetings went well, but none of them ended in an agent offer. Who knows why? Stephanie is great. She's talented, pretty, and easy to work with, but for some reason the agent always eluded her.

Regardless of the reasons, the fact still remained that Stephanie wanted an agent. So she finally began to ask for help from a few customers at the bar where she worked. Sure enough, two of them were happy to throw Stephanie a bone. They met with her immediately, made a few phone calls and set her up with multiple agent meetings. Within two days, Stephanie signed with a well-known theatrical agent who was happy to represent her. He trusted the referral he received from his colleague and Stephanie's customer, so signing her was a no-brainer.

Referrals are the mother of all ships. An industry referral provided the validation or back-up Stephanie needed to finally close the deal with an agent. Referrals will save you years of hard work and suffering.

You don't have to know any celebrities or Hollywood power players before you can gather referrals. You could get recommendations from any number of people. Start asking and see what unfolds. Your friends just might surprise you. Be willing to ask the people you know for guidance and assistance. You have nothing to lose, so buck up and ask for help. You'll be glad you did.

CHAPTER 18 DO LESS MORE OFTEN

By now I hope you're inspired to put these creative marketing principles to work. It's pretty exciting stuff and I know you're going to feel really motivated to take it all on. But don't. Really. Trust me… don't make the mistake of attempting everything at once. You're in this for the long haul, so the important element in creating a successful acting business is to create and keep good habits. Rule number one for every actor and creative entrepreneur is this, "Do less stuff more often."

Let me share a story about a client named Becky. Becky's been pursuing acting for the last three years. At this point in her career, she's shot a few independent films, had a couple of ineffective agents, met a handful of people, and now feels stuck about how to move forward because she has yet to find her "break."

There is a simple reason why Becky's not where she wants to be. She hasn't been consistent in any of her marketing or relationship-building attempts. She's tried dozens of things at one time or another and met a handful of people, but never followed up and never developed a solid marketing strategy.

I'll say it again. Rule number one for every actor and creative entrepreneur is this—DO LESS STUFF MORE OFTEN. Release the pressure of needing to do everything and replace it with a few specific and consistent actions. Send out consistent and specific ships on a regular basis so you can garner accurate and measurable results.

Successful advertisers understand an essential rule in marketing called The Rule of Seven. Basically, the average consumer doesn't absorb an advertiser's message until they've received it seven to a dozen times over the course of a few months. This is why Coca Cola spends over 85% of their money on advertising and why you often see the same Geico commercial three times in one hour. That's just the rule of seven working its magic on you.

Bed Bath and Beyond masters The Rule of Seven. Boy, if I had a dollar for every one of those blue 20% off coupons I've received! Even though I often roll my eyes when I retrieve the mail and see yet another coupon, I'll be honest with you, every time I need to buy some house wares, curtains, fans etc., I remember those coupons and happily make my way over to Bed Bath and Beyond. Though I don't use every coupon, (I mean, really, who could?), I think of Bed Bath and Beyond first when I need something.

As an actor, it is essential to apply The Rule of Seven to every aspect of your own marketing. If you want a new commercial agent, you're more likely to get a call if you target ten agencies five consecutive times rather than fifty agencies only once. Your "blue coupon" must be delivered multiple times before your consumer will feel motivated to buy.

If you want to become known by casting directors, stop trying to meet everyone and focus on a specific short list of offices that you can meet several times. That's how you become remembered. That's The Rule of Seven. Embrace it. It'll make your marketing easy and even enjoyable.

Now that you know about The Rule of Seven, I'd like to explain how to apply it to different aspects of your career. These ideas are really just suggestions to get the wheels turning in your mind. So review them, tweak them, and make them your own. Remember that there's no wrong way to achieve success in this business. You know your Tao better than anyone.

Use The Rule of Seven to Land the Right Agent

STEP ONE: CREATE YOUR TARGET LIST.

Sure, books, lists and various agency directories exist out there, but the best way to gather accurate and appropriate information about what specific agent or manager might be right for you is through word of mouth referrals. Utilize your network of people and save yourself hours of guesswork.

I recommend that you email your entire (or close to it anyway) address book to ask for ideas, referrals or thoughts about what agency might be a fit for you. Don't prejudge who may or may not be able (or willing) to offer you feedback. A recent client of mine got a strong personal recommendation to a top agency because she emailed her aunt in Florida about her agent-seeking mission. Her aunt's co-worker's cousin (yup, that's right) works for a prestigious talent agency in Los Angeles and very eagerly picked up the phone to set up a meeting for my client. You just never know. It's important that you simply request ideas or possible names rather than specific referrals in order to take any pressure off of your friends. Your email could say something like this:

Hi there! As many of you know, I am currently taking my acting career to the next level and it's time to upgrade my representation. I am in the process of reaching out to potential new agents and would love your suggestions, input and support. I really respect your opinion and would be so grateful for your valuable insight.

What specific talent agents (you don't need to know them personally, but you might know of some decent ones) might be a good fit for me? What suggestions do you have on how to best approach these potential agents?

I am open to any and all thoughts so don't be shy! Again, I truly value your input.

Many thanks!

Contrary to what you might be thinking, Your People will respond to you openly with suggestions, referrals, and maybe even phone calls from Florida. Don't judge it 'til you try it.

After you receive suggestions, do your own research. Don't forget to use imdbpro.com to locate updated information such as addresses and phone numbers in order to find out what caliber of talent each agency represents, what their general reputation is, and also who works there. Be realistic. Your goal here is to partner with an agent who will actually get you auditions, so don't limit yourself to only the top, celebrity-filled agencies. But don't sell yourself short either and target any bottom feeders out there. Focus on those agents who represent actors that are one or two steps ahead of you career wise. If your next step is booking small roles in big budget features, then target the agents who represent the actors who play those same roles.

An easy way to distinguish the right agents from the others is to also Google the agency name along with the word "complaint." If your search generates a couple of unhappy remarks, don't sweat it. But if your search generates multiple hits, I'd steer clear. No representation is better than the wrong representation. You deserve an agent who will work for you and support your efforts.

When you've decided on a short list, collect addresses and specific agent names, as well as their phone numbers and get ready to rumble. Rule of Seven Alert: Pick fewer agents than you think you should! In order for your audience (agent in this case) to absorb your message, they must receive your message seven to twelve times. Pick a manageable number of names so you can be persistent and consistent with your ships. Don't worry, after you've applied The Rule of Seven to your first group of agents, you can move on to a second short list.

STEP TWO: SEND OUT YOUR FIRST DINGY. The Rule of Seven works when your audience develops a familiarity with your product, so don't be afraid to begin with a subtle message that generates some curiosity before you send in the big guns. Your first touch might be a simple postcard, letter of interest, email, or invitation to an upcoming performance.

Step Three:	**Send out a raft.** In your second touch, I recommend highlighting a recent career success through a postcard mailing or press release.
Step Four:	**Send out a tugboat.** Enough already with the cheesy ship references! I think you get my point here. Simply put, select seven of your favorite marketing tools and send them to your target list once per week over the course of seven weeks. Here's a sample Rule of Seven Outline (minus the cheesy ship references) to illustrate my point:

Week One:	Mail a creative postcard.
Week Two:	Fax a one-sheet or press release.
Week Three:	Hand-deliver a handsome press kit.
Week Four:	Mail an enveloped postcard featuring a rave review all about you.
Week Five:	Email or deliver your demo reel.
Week Six:	Call your target list to request a meeting.
Week Seven:	Follow up with a thank you card. Even if you don't get the meeting, you can thank them for their time and consideration.

Make Workshops Work for You

How familiar does this scenario sound to you? You decide that it's time to cultivate solid relationships with television casting directors, so you sign up for a workshop service in order to meet these people face to face. Over the course of the next year, you meet two different casting directors each month totaling twenty-four first meetings. Yet no one really knows you because they've only met you once. I meet tons of actors every month who believe strongly that CD workshops don't work. Well, of course they don't when you never really develop a relationship with the casting directors you meet.

A lot of actors make this mistake and I understand why. It's easy to buy into the idea that the more people you meet, the more opportunities you'll have. But that's just not true. It's not about who you know in this town. It's about who knows you. You cannot become known after just one meeting. It takes time to build a relationship.

So here's how you can use The Rule of Seven to make casting director workshops work for you.

STEP ONE: Create your target list. There are literally hundreds of casting directors in Hollywood, so it's pretty impossible to effectively apply the Rule of Seven to all of them. Not to worry - you don't have to. Just select a small (less than 12) list of casting directors and target them specifically and consistently.

Visit www.castingabout.com or imdbpro.com and research those television shows where the most opportunity for co-stars and guest stars exists. Please note that I did not just tell you to make a list of your favorite shows! I know, everybody loves *The Office*. But part of what makes that show so great is the fact that the cast is stuck together day in and day out working in an office, so new characters are rarely introduced. Instead, make a list of those shows that feature new characters on a consistent basis such as *Cold Case*, *CSI*, or any of the other countless procedural episodics.

STEP TWO: Get some face time. Register for two different CD workshop services if you can. Now, remember, not all services are created equal. I recommend that you join a service that truly auditions their talent before accepting an actor. This insures that the caliber of talent is consistent and sets you up to really shine.

STEP THREE: Only workshop with those casting offices on your target list. This will allow you to maintain your sanity and your budget by attending a limited number of workshops with a purpose rather than taking a shot in the dark and workshopping with various CDs through a process of random selection.

STEP FOUR: Do your best to attend every workshop you can with members of your target list. Remember, it's The Rule of Seven so aim to workshop with the same people multiple times over the course of a year. That's how you become remembered. That's how you'll build trust. And that's how you'll eventually snag auditions.

STEP FIVE: Follow up. Send a thank you card after each workshop specifically speaking to one thing you appreciated or learned in the class. Be real. Be authentic. Avoid the obligatory "hey thanks... hope you call me in soon." And instead specifically identify one part of the workshop experience that you appreciated most. This shows that you actually paid attention.

STEP SIX: Stay in the loop. Send a postcard update to your target list at least every other month. Remember Bed Bath and Beyond. You must remind them how they know you and keep your name in the forefront of their minds.

STEP SEVEN: Rinse and Repeat.

You can easily apply The Rule of Seven to every area of your career. The best part about The Rule of Seven is that it allows you to become more consistent and persistent in your marketing efforts, which naturally leads to exciting results. Just remember that what you do is less important than how often you do it and how happy you are during the process. So go out there, do less stuff more often, and have a blast. It's your career, so enjoy it!

DO THE TAO

Now that you know The Rule of Seven, create a unique plan that suits your long-term vision or perhaps a short-term goal. Feel free to use my outlines for guidance, but I also invite you to make this system your own.

www.taoofshowbusiness.com/workbook.php

But, There Aren't Enough Hours in the Day!

One of the toughest things about working for yourself (which, by the way, you are doing when you pursue a career in acting) is time management. Boy, oh boy, there are millions of things you could do or should do or would do if you had the time to manage it all. Let's face it, as you are building your career, you need a day job, you need time for your craft, and you need a life. Do not allow yourself to become overwhelmed by the to-do list. This is your career. You aren't going anywhere. So trust that taking specific action each and every day will get you where you want to be. I am not suggesting that you slack off and trust in the acting Gods, but I am suggesting that success awaits you if you are willing to show up on a consistent and persistent basis. You must, must, must treat your career like any successful CEO. Show up for yourself everyday and take inspired action.

Honestly, how often have you purchased concert tickets and not attended the show? How often have you no-showed on a hair appointment or job interview? How often have you just decided not to show up for a date or skipped out on lunch plans with a friend? Huh, how often? I'm not sure why, but for some crazy reason it is often easier for most people to keep these appointments than to keep the appointments you set with yourself. Trust me, I get it. As I sit in a deserted restaurant, quarantined from the things I love most in order to finish this very book, I get it! It's called resistance and it cannot be in charge of your life.

Your job is to do the Tao and take specific consistent action toward your long-term vision as well as your short-term goals. The toughest part about finishing a project is beginning it, so create the space to begin everyday. Set some office hours and commit to working on your business on a regular basis. Don't be crazy. Begin by committing to twenty minutes of business work each day. Schedule the time and decide what specific tasks you will work on. I have found that it's easier to commit to a time frame rather than to a specific result, so break your work into twenty-minute intervals. Don't worry, you can work longer if you choose, but it's easier to commit to just twenty minutes than to find a few hours to block off each day. How can you say no to twenty short minutes?

I had the opportunity to coach two different screenwriters during the same timeframe. Both writers wanted to complete a screenplay and both struggled to begin the project because the thought of writing an entire script was overwhelming. Both writers developed a writing schedule in order to complete their scripts. One set aside six hours every Friday to write. He figured that by clocking six hours each week, the script would be completed in a matter of weeks. The funny thing was that the reality of having six hours in a row to write was a tough commitment to keep. One week, he had out of town visitors, another week he had to fill in for a sick coworker. Week after week, obstacles popped up that prevented him from keeping his six-hour commitment. He often thought, "Well, without an entire six hours to commit, why bother even getting started?"

The other writer decided she would simply write a page every day. Some days she literally hand wrote one sentence in giant font to fulfill her page-a-day commitment. But on most days, after completing the first page, the second one quickly followed, then the third, then the fourth. At the end of only four weeks, writer number two had a completed script in her hands, while poor writer number one had only clocked in six hours of writing time.

You see, it's easier to take action on a simple goal such as writing a page rather than carving out an entire day to pound out some hard work. The same is true when it comes to sending out your ships and managing your acting business. It's easier to send out five postcards each day rather than 150 in one sitting. It's easier to self-submit each morning for five minutes rather than once a week for an hour.

Break your office hours into small segments that are easier to say yes to than to resist. I urge you to create a work schedule and mark your commitment in your calendar. Clock in and clock out. Track your progress. The hardest part is starting. Start small so you can finish big.

DO THE TAO

Pull out your day planner and book yourself at least twenty minutes each day to work your acting business.

www.taoofshowbusiness.com/workbook.php

PLAY TIME

Like I said earlier, *The Tao of Show Business* requires a balance between external work and internal focus; between work and play. This entire section of the book has been about work, work, and work. Now, at last you get to play!

While you're out there making big things happen, it's important to take time to play, be creative, and stay on track by infusing some artistic energy into your to-do list. Though I know your career is serious stuff, you don't have to take it so darn seriously all the time. Have some fun and play with the results you're trying to obtain.

I coached an actor named Martin who planned to book a role on his favorite TV series. He worked hard each day doing all the work required to make this happen and though he made progress, he had successfully sucked every last ounce of joy out of his journey. All work and no play made Martin no fun to be around, so he decided to play with what his future might look like. He created a GQ magazine cover with his face on the front. He also created a Broadway playbill starring none other than Martin, of course! He even created new closing credits to his favorite film to include his name. Martin just had some fun playing with his future and balancing all his hard work with fun energy.

You can play with what your future looks like, too. Pretend that you're famous for a day and try leaving your house looking paparazzi-ready. Sign, frame, and mount your headshot on the wall. Design your future cover of *Entertainment Weekly*. Host an awards show in your living room. Write that acceptance speech. Journal about what it's like to work with Ron Howard. If you haven't already done so, create that Vision Board I mentioned in Chapter 3 of this book. Rather than just monotonously submitting yourself online, pretend that you're reviewing movie offers and decide which film will be your next one. Just play a little, stop being so serious, have some fun, and bring evidence of your future into your life today. Go on...do it.

You are well on your way to mastering *The Tao of Show Business*. You're describing your vision along with your goals, you're declaring and sharing your mission with the Collaborators in your life, and you're taking inspired and consistent action. What else can there possibly be?

The final element in *The Tao of Show Business* cycle is development. To live the Tao means to go with the flow, change with the times, and adjust when you need. When you develop the Tao, you do just that. You develop your process and change your plans while you're living out the life you imagine.

The Tao of Development is serious business. Here's where you really face your fears and create change. This is the place where you become a better form of you; where you overcome obstacles, and define your own place in this business. Here's where you get to teach other actors everything you know. Here's where the fun really begins.

When you arrive at the development phase of your Tao, your relationships change dramatically, you come into your own, and you create everlasting satisfaction in more than just your acting career.

Welcome to your Tao. Your journey is almost done.

STAY FLEXIBLE

It was Albert Einstein who said, "The definition of insanity is doing the same thing over and over again and expecting different results." Every action you take produces a result. In *The Tao of Show Business*, your job is to take an objective look at the results you produce and make the necessary adjustments before taking the next action. If you audition countless times without producing a callback, it's time to adjust how you approach auditions. If your current headshots look great, but don't produce auditions, it's time to re-evaluate your photos. If you've been with the same manager or acting coach for years yet your career hasn't changed, it might be time to shake up your team a little. If you can't seem to catch a break doing what you're doing, it's time to do it differently. It's not time to quit, but it is time to avoid insanity. In order to create the career of your dreams, you must be willing to take action, to try new things, and to make some mistakes along the way.

Let me be crystal clear here. I am in no way suggesting that you jump around giving up on things before they have time to develop. I am also not suggesting that you quit when the going gets rough. I am simply reminding you to stay alert and open to making changes. Be flexible in your actions and willing to adjust the plan as things unfold. That's all.

Flexibility can help you to avoid failure. Please know however, that failure itself is not actually real. Dr. Wayne Dyer discusses failure in his book, *Ten Secrets for Success and Inner Peace.* He writes, "This may come as a surprise to you, but failure is an illusion. No one ever fails at anything. Everything you do produces a result."

It's impossible for you to fail at anything because everything you do simply produces a result. So then, what will you do with the results that you generate? Will you quit or beat yourself up when an audition goes south? Will you tell yourself that you aren't cut out for this business after your first rejection?

Martin Scorsese finally won an Oscar for his film, *The Departed,* in 2007. Does that make all his other films failures? Does it even mean that *The Departed* was his best piece of work? Michelle Kwan entered the 1998 Olympics as a World Champion Figure Skater and the gold medal favorite. But the gold slipped through her fingers and she won the silver instead. Does that make her a figure skating failure? Babe Ruth holds the Major League baseball record for most strike outs, yet he is known as one of baseball's greatest legends rather than a failure. You see, failure is just an idea. It's only a judgment, and it doesn't have to exist in your acting journey.

A client named Grant is a full time commercial actor who has worked consistently over the course of about fifteen years. One day, Grant fell flat on his face during an audition. Not literally, but he may as well have… it was that bad. After slinking out of the room, Grant hopped in his car where his friend awaited him. Feeling like a failure, Grant complained to his friend, "It's just not worth it. I'm not any good at this. I guess I'm not really meant to be an actor."

Luckily, Grant's friend was much less dramatic and quickly knocked some sense into Grant. He said, "Excuse me, but if I am not mistaken you've already won at this acting thing. How many more people do you think move to a city where an acting career is possible, but go home after a short time? How many other people live here and say they're doing this acting thing, but don't study or workshop or attempt to improve their craft? You're already successful. You've already won. Everything from here is just part of that."

Thanks, Grant's friend. I couldn't have said it better myself!

Just like Grant, you, too, have already made it. You're here, you're doing this, and you're getting better. Most importantly, you're willing to move through setbacks and perceived failures along your journey toward acting success. Failure is a fake out. It's just a tricky form of resistance. Don't fall victim to it.

If failure isn't actually real, then neither is perfection. They are both ideas about good and bad or about right and wrong. Neither concept really serves you. Perfectionism can distract you from taking action and being happy with your career. When you strive for perfection, knowing it isn't real, you simply set yourself up for disappointment.

I worked with an actor named Emma who had hit a plateau in her career. Emma felt stuck and unmotivated. She knew what she needed to do, but for some reason couldn't manage to ever get it done. You see, Emma suffered from a little thing called perfectionism and it paralyzed her.

Emma needed new headshots, but wanted to lose ten pounds before re-shooting. She wanted to find the perfect agent, but didn't know who that person was yet. She wanted to complete a postcard mailing, but didn't know what message to write. She wanted to join a networking group, but couldn't decide which one would be best for her.

I asked Emma what stopped her from pursuing representation. She told me that she was afraid of signing with the wrong agent. I asked her what prevented her from testing out the networking waters. She replied that she felt overwhelmed by too many options and didn't want to end up at the wrong place.

Emma's desire for the perfect career, the perfect agent, and the perfect networking group prevented her from taking any action. Her belief in perfection and failure wasn't working for her. She was so afraid that she might make a mistake that she didn't do anything.

I decided that Emma needed to free herself from her need for perfection. Perfection, just like failure, isn't real. It's just an idea about how things should be or what they could look like. But it doesn't actually exist. When you attempt to attain this thing that is completely unattainable, you're bound to lose motivation, feel discouraged, or even throw in the towel.

Perfectionism is shrewd. It's the ultimate form of resistance. It's just a fancy way to avoid being truly accountable. When you insist on perfect results, you provide yourself with an out. Why take any action if it can't be perfect, right?

In order to have the career you really desire, you must be willing to practice imperfection. This is precisely what I encouraged Emma to do. So, for the next several weeks, Emma began to practice imperfection.

Playing with imperfection opened Emma up to new possibilities. It also transformed her career. She began networking. Yes, she found a few networking groups that weren't her style, but soon enough she found the "perfect" group for her. She discovered it only because she was willing to find some wrong groups first.

Emma decided to mail her imperfect headshots out to fifty agents whose names she literally drew from a hat. Two days after the mailing went out, she received a call from a top commercial agency and had a meeting set up for the following week.

Emma busted out of her rut when she practiced imperfection. She learned that the more willing she was to make mistakes, the more easily she found what was right for her. She understood that the path to a "perfect" career included some rather imperfect steps. She realized that perfectionism only kept her stuck.

You can eliminate failure by practicing imperfection. In order to take your career to the heights you are capable of, you must release any need for perfection and get used to making mistakes. The only way to really succeed at something is to be willing to be bad at it first. That's how you learn. That's how you get better.

The next time you are paralyzed by ideas of failure or perfection, ask yourself, "What do I need to do to find out if I'm right?" Then be open to finding out. If you fear your postcards won't work, what do you need to do to find out if that's true? You must mail your postcards. If you fear that your headshots are bad, what do you need to do in order to find out just how bad they are? Show them to people and get some feedback. If you fear that you're horrible at improv, what do you need to do in order to find out? Well, try some improv. The cure to perfectionism and to a fear of failure is to do it anyway. Take action, practice imperfection, and grow from there.

United Technologies Corporation published the following message in the Wall Street Journal in 1981:

You've failed many times although you may not remember.
You fell down the first time you tried to walk.
You almost drowned the first time you tried to swim, didn't you?
Did you hit the ball the first time you swung a bat?
Heavy hitters, the ones who hit the most home runs, also strike out a lot.
RH Macy failed seven times before his store in New York caught on.
English novelist John Creasey got 753 rejection slips before he published 564 books.
Babe Ruth struck out 1330 times, but he also hit 714 home runs.
Don't worry about failure.
Worry about the chances you miss when you don't even try.

Failure ceases to exist when you let go of perfectionism. Now you just get to play and be curious about how great things can really be. Besides, you might really surprise yourself when you produce results far beyond what you could ever expect or plan.

My sister, Tracy, is a stupendous mom. She's the best. When Tracy's daughters were born, my sister really wanted them to be good at everything. She wanted Keauna and Kelsie to throw softballs correctly, to color in the lines, to read well, to sing in tune, and to be the best they could be. So Tracy tried to help her daughters grow into perfect people. It didn't really go according to plan. The girls liked coloring outside the lines and they weren't at all interested in softball. Tracy quickly figured out that when she stepped out of her daughters' way and accepted whatever failures might come, Keauna and Kelsie became the most amazing little girls. They are different in every way, yet both girls are pretty darn perfect. When Tracy let go of her idea of perfection, the result was something far greater than she could have ever expected.

You can have a *perfect* career free of any failures when you decide to let go, be flexible and learn from every experience you encounter.

DEVELOP THE TAO

Release your need for perfection. For the next two weeks, do something imperfectly each day. Come on. Live a little dangerously!

www.taoofshowbusiness.com/workbook.php

Stop, Drop, Dig and Roll

Sure, being flexible is easy when you've got time to think about it. But what about when disaster strikes or when you find yourself in an emergency situation? The Stop, Drop, Dig and Roll is not some fancy dance move. It's an easy way to step out of crisis and back into taking care of business. It'll take some practice, but you can move through any disaster pretty easily when you follow these four steps.

STEP ONE: Stop! Stop what you're doing and take five while you gather yourself. You won't move through this crisis if you're stuck in crazy-town, so just stop for a minute.

Perhaps your agent gets you an audition while you are out of town. With all of the chaos prior to the trip, you forgot to book out with your agent before you left and now she's not very happy that you can't make this audition.

STEP TWO: Drop your story. Drop the dramatic details so you can just focus on the facts of the situation.

Do not focus on the drama around your situation. You could spend countless hours complaining and worrying about how this one mistake might ruin your career. You could wonder if your agent will drop you off her roster. You could lament over how scatter-brained you are. You could go on and on for hours reviewing every detail and filling yourself with regret and worry.

You must let go of this crazy-talk because none of it will help you find a resolution. Your story, though interesting, only keeps you stuck.

STEP THREE: Dig a little deeper. Why does this matter to you? Why is this an emergency? After you've separated the facts from fiction, identify what values or priorities you hold that make this situation a crisis.

The missed audition highlights the fact that you value your acting career. You want to seize every opportunity that comes your way. It also highlights how much you value solid communication with your agent.

STEP FOUR: Roll with your values. Don't worry about the fiction or even the facts for that matter. Focusing on your commitments, decide what actions you can take to move out of breakdown mode and into breakthrough mode.

Understanding that career and communication are your top priorities, you can now decide to set up a meeting with your agent when you arrive to town. You can create a protocol for booking out, or you could even hop on the next plane back to Hollywood to make the audition after all.

You can take any number of actions in line with your values. You can do so quickly and easily when you let go of the emotions or fiction behind your emergency and just focus on what matters most.

The Stop, Drop, Dig and Roll should help you steer clear of blocks in emergency situations. It'll force you to let go of the drama easily and deal with what's really going on.

DEVELOP THE TAO

Think about a recent crisis or emergency you experienced and apply the Stop, Drop, Dig and Roll to uncover an easier way to live.

www.taoofshowbusiness.com/workbook.php

PRACTICE PATIENCE

THE SECOND IMPORTANT ASPECT TO THE TAO OF Development involves patience. I know, I know, you've been told this a million times, but it's true. You must be patient while you pursue your dream. Patience is indeed a virtue and it's one that ironically becomes more challenging to master the closer you get to the finish line.

Develop the Habit

It has been said that it takes 21 days to form a habit. In order to increase your chances of success and avoid show business burnout, you must commit to habits rather than attach to any specific result. You must practice patience.

You cannot control when your agent will call, when you'll get your big break, or how often those residual checks come in, but you can control your own daily activity. Commit to developing the habits of a successful and balanced lifestyle. This goes back to The Rule of Seven. No one thing you do will make or break you, but you can create success by consistently doing one thing each day.

Poet and writer, Ian Krieger, wrote the following about our friend, Mr. Habit.

> I *am your constant companion.*
> *I am your greatest helper or heaviest burden.*
> *I will push you onward or drag you down to failure.*
> *I am completely at your command.*
> *Half of the things you do you might as well turn over to me*
> *and I will do them-quickly and correctly.*
> *I am easily managed – you must be firm with me.*
> *Show me exactly how you want something done and*
> *after a few lessons, I will do it automatically.*
> *I am the servant of great people, and alas of all failures as well.*
> *Those who are failures, I have made failures.*
> *I am not a machine though I work with the precision of a machine*
> *plus the intelligence of a person.*
> *You may run me for profit or run me for ruin –*
> *it makes no difference to me.*
> *Take me, train me, be firm with me and*
> *I will place the world at your feet.*
> *Be easy with me and I will destroy you.*
> *Who am I?*
> *I am habit.*

My client, Marissa, really wanted to book a guest star role on a network television series. This goal seemed somewhat challenging to her, but the prospect of breaking out of her co-star rut and into the guest star level really thrilled her. Marissa created a plan and went all out in her efforts to achieve this goal within thirty days. For the first two weeks of her plan, Marissa did everything she could to make the guest star thing happen. She worked hard, she self-submitted, she told everyone she could about her intention, and she continued to feel excited.

Then week three came and with the looming deadline quickly approaching, Marissa began to feel discouraged because she had not yet booked her guest star role. Soon her efforts and focus slowed down and eventually crept to a stop. At the end of her 30-day deadline, Marissa decided she had failed. Period. No guest star for her. Bummer.

The mistake Marissa made was to cling desperately to the deadline and timeline rather than just commit to developing the habit of taking steady action everyday toward her desires. She became attached to extremely high expectations instead of committing to the vision of her greatest desires. She did not allow herself the opportunity to form the daily habit of work. She became impatient and distracted by perceived results.

Though deadlines do work to motivate you and create accountability, they can also become a distraction. Marissa's deadline distracted her from her commitment to her acting career as a whole. She put so much meaning and pressure on her timeline, that it left her little room for error or exploration.

Marissa agreed to try something new. She dropped this thirty-day guest star goal and replaced it with the commitment to take five specific steps each day toward booking a guest star. The actions involved in both goals stayed the same, but with a shift in her perspective, Marissa focused on maintaining her momentum and creating the habit of working hard.

Wouldn't you know it! Over the next four weeks, Marissa booked the lead in an independent film, she booked another co-star role on her favorite series and began auditioning for guest star roles for the first time in her career. Marissa now knows that regardless of when she books her first guest star, the only thing standing between her and that goal is time.

Most of the time, deadlines work to motivate you and keep you on track. But don't be fooled by their importance. In truth, a deadline is just a mile marker or measuring stick. They're something you decide on. They're also something you can change. Use deadlines to stay in momentum, but don't allow them to rule your life.

The only place of power is in the present moment. Marissa could not change the past, she could not predict the future, all she could do was attend to the situation at hand and embrace patience in that moment, on that day.

What's happening right now in your career? What do you choose to do about it? How can you maintain your goals and action plans all while staying focused on the present day? The key is to notice when you are distracted by worry and impatience. Notice when you focus more on what might happen than on what's actually happening. Pay attention to how often you regret past mistakes or decisions. You cannot know what you do not know, so stay present and open to what's coming. You cannot change your past regardless of how much you worry about it. To control your career and develop your Tao, you must be willing to stay present and develop successful habits.

An easy way to set yourself up for success in this area is to create an accountability system to keep you on track and motivated. Here are a few fun suggestions:

Create a Tip Jar. Money talks, so reward yourself when you keep your commitment. Let's say you want to book a guest star too, so you commit to devoting one hour of work toward this goal each day. Every time you keep that commitment, you can tip yourself three bucks. The dollar amount doesn't really matter here, but I recommend making the amount small enough to afford but also large enough to matter to you.

Sounds fun, huh? Well, on the days you don't keep your commitment you must remove three dollars from your tip jar and donate it to a charity of your choice. Not so fun. Knowing you must part with cold hard cash is a fantastic incentive to keep your word.

At the end of a month (or specific time period of your choice) you get to empty your tip jar and reward yourself by spending the dough on a lovely treat: a massage, a dinner out, a bottle of gin, whatever suits your fancy.

Pick a Partner. Accountability is a lovely thing, so invite a friend to help you stay on track. The two of you can commit to check in at the end of each day and report on the actions you took for that day as well as your plans for the coming day. Just knowing that someone will be expecting a report on your work will keep you going. I once had two students agree to hold each other accountable to complete three tasks per day toward their acting business - one before 10:00 am, one before 1:00 pm, and the last before 5:00pm. At each designated time, they sent a text message to each other just to say, "Yup. Got my ten o'clock done." Over a very short time frame, they each made significant progress towards their career goals thanks to their buddy system.

Hire a Career Coach. As a coach, I understand the value of coaching. I myself often work with a coach of my own. A coach will not only create intense accountability for you, but your coach will also raise the bar and really push you to expand your personal realm of possibility. Also, there is something to be said about the power of financially investing in yourself. If you are paying someone to assist you in achieving your personal and professional goals, trust me you will make sure you get your money's worth by following through on your commitments. Your coach will present you with new ideas or methods for accomplishing your goals. Your coach will also empower you to take bold risks and encourage you to challenge yourself. Coaches assist you to break out of old, ugly habits and overcome other personal blocks. Coaches rule!

Celebrate Your Progress. With all this focus on your to-do list and what is left undone, it's easy to forget about your successes along the way. I don't know about you, but when it comes to my to-do list, every time I check something off, I add even more tasks to the bottom of the list. My to-do list becomes the never-ending log of what I haven't done yet. That's fine and all, but come on! When do you get to celebrate those things you've actually finished? Where is the focus on the accomplishments? Don't wait until you're an Oscar winner to celebrate your life! Try keeping a success journal. Write down five of the day's accomplishments each night before you go to sleep. Sometimes your accomplishments might be award-winning, other times they might be very simple. It doesn't matter. An accomplishment exists when you are willing to own it and celebrate it. So celebrate the journey. It'll make the ride a lot more fun!

DEVELOP THE TAO

Create your accountability system and go for it!

www.taoofshowbusiness.com/workbook.php

Change for a Change

Over the years, I've witnessed my students completely transform their lives during my six-week Career Cooperative Workshop. I'll be honest with you; a lot of times it ain't pretty. But then again, change never is. When you commit to changing your career for the better, you can expect to go through quite a learning curve on your way to success. That's just what change looks like. It's messy. It's uncomfortable. It's awkward and it doesn't necessarily feel good. Change brings a lot of stuff to the surface, that's for sure. Change also creates an enormous feeling of impatience because you just want the results, not all the uncomfortable gunk that comes with it.

I mentioned this example earlier, but if you want to lose fifty pounds, you must first lose one, then another, then a few more. During the weight-loss process, your weight will probably bounce around and plateau for a while before you hit your goal weight. That's the way weight loss works. It's not a linear process, but if you want to lose all fifty pounds, you must go through the ups and downs on your way to your ideal weight.

Change itself is not linear or orderly or precise. You're moving into uncharted territory, so expect some bumps and bruises along the way. That's change for ya! But you can't accomplish your long-term career vision without change. You must be willing to change and be patient during the process in order to make your wildest dreams come true. So, how about it? Are you ready to change for a change?

Let me share a secret with you to help you deal with change a little more gracefully. It's called psycho-cybernetics and it's more than just a Scrabble-winning word. Psycho-cybernetics essentially explains why change is so tough. When you understand it, you'll be able to embrace the process of change more easily.

A cybernetic mechanism is a little doohickey designed to maintain the status quo of a particular environment such as a filter in a fish tank or a thermostat in a room. If your bedroom thermostat is set at seventy-one degrees and you open the windows one fine November morning, the heat will kick into high gear keeping the room's temperature at the standard seventy-one degrees. That's just the thermostat, or cybernetic mechanism doing its job.

You've got your own thermostat and it's called a psycho-cybernetic mechanism. Its sole purpose is to maintain whatever temperature (or comfort level) you are used to, even if your comfort level is not the most desirable of circumstances. So, if you've always been broke, your thermostat is set at "broke." If you've never booked a guest-star role, your thermostat is set at "no guest-stars." This means that when you begin to make changes, your psycho-cybernetic mechanism will kick in and attempt to prevent the temperature change within you.

Your thermostat is very advanced and it will do whatever it takes to maintain the temperature at which it's been programmed. So when you begin to change your personal temperature, you can expect the heat to blast down on you. That's the process of change. Never fear, though, because just like a thermostat in a room, you can alter the setting of your internal thermostat. It takes a little effort and a lot of patience, but it is indeed possible.

For Marissa, things got tough while she went from a no guest star setting to a guest star setting. She didn't know about psycho-cybernetics so she made the mistake of calling it quits when the heat came. Marissa misread the heat as failure, when in fact it was serving as a sign that change was on its way. She eventually figured it out and ultimately changed her cybernetic setting. Cool, huh?

You can do it, too. It's actually pretty easy. All you have to do is absolutely nothing. When you are in the process of change, your only job is to stay there. When things get tough and the going gets rough, you don't need to do anything more than lean forward into your new setting.

The next time you experience impatience or frustration with your progress, celebrate it rather than jump ship. That discomfort is just your psycho-cybernetic mechanism kicking in which means change is on the way. Just sit tight and understand that change is not linear. You're not failing; you're changing. If you can hang on through the discomfort of change you will ultimately reprogram your internal thermostat to match the future life you want for yourself.

What You Resist, Persists

Now that you know all about psycho-cybernetics, let's take a look at resistance itself. Resistance is that strong force that slows your progress down. Sometimes it might be an anxious or fearful feeling. Sometimes, it might look like bad luck. Resistance might be an excuse you make or an objection you have. Resistance may seem silly or make a lot of sense. Resistance is fear, procrastination, laziness, hyper-activity, and insecurity. Any way you slice it, resistance just works to keep you from living the life you desire.

Resistance can be powerful, even paralyzing, but it is a natural occurrence for every actor, or human being for that matter. A lot of my clients want to figure out why they resist certain actions or where their resistance originates. Though this can be valuable information, it's not essential to overcoming resistance itself. You can spend a lot of energy exploring the resistance or you can use that same energy to take action and overcome whatever thoughts, feelings, or distractions that might hold you back.

Resistance is natural. It shows up when you're about to do something new or something important to you. You don't have to be free of resistance completely before you take action. You don't have to beat your resistance before you can get where you want to go. You don't have to judge yourself just because you feel resistance. Instead, you can be grateful for the strong emotions reminding you that what you are about to do matters to you.

I coached a client named Autumn who had a list of industry referrals she wanted to call in hopes of securing a great manager. She knew the calls would get her somewhere because they came from reliable and respected people in the business. Every week, she committed to making the calls and every week she just couldn't bring herself to do it. Autumn was is full resistance-mode and she was completely frustrated with herself for giving in to the resistance. She wondered why the phone calls were so difficult to make. Autumn felt that she had to pummel her resistance into submission before she could move forward at all.

Autumn focused so intently on her resistance and her judgment around it that she forgot all about the calls she intended to make. She treated resistance as her enemy and frankly resistance was winning this battle big time. Autumn resisted calling prospective managers simply because having a manager was important to her. Her resistance just shined a light on how high the stakes were for Autumn when it came to picking up the phone.

Though resistance isn't fun, it is not the enemy. It can be a distraction though. Autumn viewed resistance as some form of weakness, so she focused on beating the resistance rather than making her calls. She tried to cure herself of resistance before she could move forward. Ironically though, the only way she could actually overcome her own resistance was to pick up the phone and take action regardless of how strong her resistance was.

Which is exactly what she did in the end. Autumn stopped judging her resistance and started using it as a motivator. When she ceased to judge her resistance, she was no longer paralyzed by it. Resistance no longer controlled her or distracted her from the task at hand.

Now when Autumn feels nervous, fearful, distracted or unsure, she knows her resistance is just popping up to remind her that her career matters. So naturally, she might feel this way.

When you're nervous before an audition or performance, it's not a sign that you're some sort of amateur. It's actually a sign that you care about the outcome. When you don't really feel like putting up that difficult scene in class, you're no chicken. You're probably excited about the challenge or nervous about the risk. When you avoid finishing projects, you're not lazy. You're just unsure of what might come next. Nerves are natural, so is resistance.

So, what do you do with your resistance? Do you fight it or judge it? Do you allow it to distract you from the important steps you could be taking? Or do you use that energy to catapult yourself to new heights? You can feel resistance without succumbing to it.

Did you know that your body experiences fear and excitement in the same way? The goose bumps, the rolling stomach, the sweaty palms, and the rapid heartbeat are all signs of fear as much as they are of excitement. Picture something that really scares you such as calling an agent, performing stand-up—anything will do. Now, notice the physical response in your body. Notice your breathing and your heart rate. Notice which parts of your body get tense and alert.

Next, picture something that really excites you, like winning an Oscar or working with your dream director. Notice the physical response in your body now. You'll find it's pretty much the same. Though your body can't tell the difference between fear and excitement, your mind sure seems to think it can. When you label an emotion as fear, you are bound to experience resistance, which ultimately distracts you from the task at hand.

Robert Heller said, "Fear is excitement without breath." So the next time you feel fear or resistance, thank your body for showing you that this thing you fear is important to you then reframe the fear as excitement and take the action anyway. Use that energy to keep you moving rather than keep you stuck. Resistance is a gift, so feel the fear and do it anyway.

DEVELOP THE TAO

Make a list of at least three actions you've been resisting. For seven days, do one thing that scares you. Live a little dangerously.

www.taoofshowbusiness.com/workbook.php

IT TAKES SOME TRUST

ALONG WITH FLEXIBILITY AND PATIENCE, THE TAO of Development requires some serious trust. You must trust yourself during your journey, even when things don't look the way you thought they would. You must trust in your own decisions enough to know when to change your mind or make adjustments. You must trust that you are doing your job to the best of your abilities and trust that others are doing the same. You must trust in your long-term vision and know that each step you take brings you one step closer to living the career of your dreams. *The Tao of Show Business* outlines a path to success and fulfillment in this industry, but only you can know your way. Trust yourself to discover and master your own perfect path.

Besides, the opinions of others are really none of your business. You can meet with the industry's most powerful talent agent who shares with you all her secrets to how this business really works. Though some or even most of the insight may resonate with you, you cannot expect or allow these words of wisdom to directly apply to you in your own journey. That's just not how it works. I said it before, and I'll say it again: there is no single set path to success in this business. So eat the fish and spit out the bones. Take what resonates and test it out while you toss aside whatever doesn't work for you. Now, that's the Tao.

Do Whatever You Want

Yeah, that's right. I said it. Go and do whatever you want to do. I dare you. You might be surprised to learn that what you want to do is actually in line with your highest good, so go for it. Do whatever you want. I know, there's a lot of stuff you're supposed to do on a daily basis in order to make this whole acting thing happen. But who wants to do what they're supposed to do all the time? It's no fun working under obligation. Doing so often leads to boredom, loss of energy or even career paralysis. Trust your gut and do what you want.

Last year, an actress named Bobbi hired me to help her find some motivation. She's a busy person with a lot going on. She's not only an actor, but she's also a writer and stand-up comedian with quite an interesting social life. Needless to say, Bobbi's calendar is a full one. With such a busy schedule full of appointments and obligations, Bobbi was drained and lacked any passion for her career. Simply put, the girl was overwhelmed and exhausted. With so many projects going on, Bobbi couldn't devote sufficient energy to anything she worked on. She was spread too thin. Bobbi felt like she wasn't good at anything because she couldn't effectively throw her energy in a million and one different directions.

Digging a little deeper, I discovered that Bobbi treated everything she did as an obligation rather than a choice. She believed that she had to work really hard in order to make it. She believed she had to stay super busy every day. If she didn't, somehow that meant she wasn't going to be successful. Bobbi stayed really busy doing the essential stuff she knew she was supposed to do, but nowhere did she find the time to do what she wanted. She also had a hard time saying no, which wasn't really working for her either. It's no wonder that Bobbi lost steam.

So, I challenged Bobbi to try a little experiment. For two weeks, Bobbi agreed to do only those things she really wanted to do. She agreed to wake up each morning and ask herself, "What do I want to do today?" Her answer would then dictate how she spent her time.

This idea made Bobbi pretty nervous. She feared that if left to her own devices, she'd just stay in bed eating pizza, watching *Sex in the*

City reruns and ignoring her career. But she agreed that her old way of doing things wasn't working, so she'd give it a whirl.

What happened next was pretty cool. Bobbi was right. She did spend close to two full days just hanging out, pigging out, and watching television. She soon grew tired of that, so she dug out an old, unfinished script and began work on it. Over the next few days, she continued to do whatever she wanted and she got tons of stuff done. Not only did she finish the script, but she also joined an improv group, made some agent calls, ate great food, and got a more flexible day job. Bobbi stopped hanging out with the wrong people, she began attending regular yoga class, and started cooking at home for fun. When Bobbi consciously chose how to spend her time, she realized that her choices were absolutely in line with her highest good.

Owning her choices, she fully enjoyed everything she did free of guilt or obligation. When Bobbi compared her list of obligations to her list of want-to-dos, she discovered that the lists weren't that different. Knowing she could choose her tasks, she was once again in charge of her life. Even when she ate pizza in bed, she loved it and owned that decision as well. Life for Bobbi became fun, productive, and empowering.

Bobbi felt liberated and in command because her career belonged to her once again. She could indeed do anything she wanted to do and what she really wanted to do was creatively and aggressively pursue her acting and screenwriting career.

What would be different about your career if you only did those things you absolutely wanted to do? How would you approach your to-do list if it only contained tasks you truly desired to take on? How might you feel about your life if you lived each day exactly according to your inner most desires? What would it take to trust yourself enough to take complete ownership of your choices, your actions, and your results?

DEVELOP THE TAO

Do whatever you want... just for a week.
Watch what happens.

www.taoofshowbusiness.com/workbook.php

Get Your Priorities Straight

If just doing whatever you want freaks you out too much, then try prioritizing your obligations in a way that frees you up to focus on what's most important while alleviating any guilt about what you're not doing.

You're a creative genius with lots of irons in the fire. Multi-tasking is great, but sometimes it's also a fantastic way to avoid ever finishing anything. Try approaching your career with laser beam focus rather than leaf blower focus and start prioritizing your actions in order to finally finish some stuff. You can work on twelve projects at a time and inch your way along with each one for months without making much progress. Or you can hone in on a small handful of projects and really generate incredible results. So, here's a little trick to help you easily prioritize your schedule and make the most out of your time.

STEP ONE: Write a complete list of all the tasks you currently do, you should do, you'd like to do, or you must do. Your list might look something like this:

finish one-man show script
secure a good manager
exercise every day
cook dinner at home
send marketing email out to Hit List and Fan Club
attend four casting workshops per month
meditate
journal every morning
research network executives

STEP TWO: On a scale of 1 to 10 (1 being least urgent and 10 being most urgent) please rate how important or urgent each individual task is to you in the next thirty days. Don't worry about comparing each item with the others on the list. Just rate them all on their own merits. You may end up with thirty 7s, which is perfectly okay. Your ratings could look like this:

finish one-man show script 10
secure a good manager 8
exercise every day 8
cook dinner at home 3
send marketing email out to Hit List and Fan Club 5
attend four casting workshops per month 7
meditate 8
journal every morning 5
research network executives 3

STEP THREE: Take a look at your list and decide which tasks you can put on the back burner for the next month. I'd recommend shelving anything that does not make at least a 4 rating. Don't worry! You can revisit these tasks next month. The goal here is to clear your plate and get stuff done. You're amazing and will eventually complete the entire list, so let's just make it easier on you. Your revised list could be:

finish one-man show script 10
secure a good manager 8
exercise every day 8
attend four casting workshops per month 7
meditate 8

STEP FOUR: After you've dropped the less urgent matters, you might notice that you feel liberated or energized to tackle the more pressing items. What a relief to not have to cook at home more, right? Now, decide on an appropriate action you can take that matches the level of importance or urgency for each task. Looking at the tens on your list, ask yourself, "What is a level 10 action I can take toward completing this project?" The key here is to commit enough time, energy, or focus to match the level of importance you place on each project. Here's a sample:

Finish one-man show script
Write for ninety minutes each morning and set a deadline with my friend to create accountability.

Secure a good manager
Email my friends for referrals or recommendations and hand-deliver my headshots to at least 18 managers.

Exercise every day
Go back to working out with my trainer.

Attend four casting workshops per month
Reserve my seat in at least two before the end of the week.

Meditate
Register for Meditation for Beginners class and complete the course.

STEP FIVE: Go do it. Keep your commitments and get the important stuff done and dusted.

DEVELOP THE TAO

Check out the Priority Assignment in your *The Tao of Show Business Companion Workbook.*

www.taoofshowbusiness.com/workbook.php

Should-ing Never Helped Anybody

A big part of trust comes down to maintaining a keen awareness of choice. That's really what all this Tao talk is about – choice. What else is there, really? When you develop an awareness of choice, you maintain power and confidence in all that you do. When you forget that you do indeed choose your path, things get all mixed up, crazy and confused as you lose sight of what you can and cannot control.

Let's talk about my least favorite word in the English language. This word is used all too often and it's one that immediately strips you of an awareness of choice. The word is "should" and it can often lead you down a slippery slope to Crazyville. *Should* is dangerous because the word itself implies good and bad, right and wrong. *Should* often accompanies judgment or regret and easily distracts you from the task at hand.

You cannot regret anything strongly enough in order to reverse the past. You cannot beat yourself up enough to raise yourself to the level of success that lies within you. You cannot *should* yourself enough to ever embrace empowered actions for your career. *Should* never helped anybody and when you *should* your career away, you lose any option for change.

Daniel, a thirty-something year old actor and client of mine came to me one day feeling like a loser. Here he was well into his thirties and still, he wasn't acting full-time. Daniel was deep into *should*-mode regretting his late start in the business, his lack of focus over the years, his missed opportunities, you name it – he regretted it. Daniel believed wholeheartedly that he *should* be successful already and the fact that he wasn't must mean he was doomed.

So here he was, *should-ing* his time away and focusing only on what could have, should have, or would have been. Daniel felt powerless and frustrated. He was stuck in the muck of his beliefs and regrets, leaving him no choice for the future.

Author and speaker, Byron Katie, discusses the pitfalls of the word *should* in her book, *Loving What Is*. In it, she urges her readers to let go of their belief that any circumstance *should* look any different than it does right in that moment. She explains that your beliefs and your *shoulds* are what create stress in your life. When you let go of *should*, you can deal with the reality at hand, restoring a sense of choice.

The truth of the matter is that Daniel *shouldn't* be more successful than he is right now. That's true because he just isn't more successful. He is where he is until he isn't there any longer. His résumé has five credits on it until it has six. He doesn't book jobs until he then books a job. Judging himself and his career, Daniel just suffered and lost focus on what was possible for the future. By believing his *shoulds*, Daniel bought into the idea that he was a failure and had no choice but to continue to fail.

By finally accepting that *should*-ing only kept him stuck, Daniel began to accept the truth of his career, which was that, in this moment, he's not yet successful. But he could be. Daniel replaced his *should* with a *could* and immediately restored his awareness of choice. With the idea that he *could* be more successful in the future, Daniel felt motivated to then pursue his future success rather than regret the past.

Do not fall victim to your beliefs about how things should look. You are exactly where you *should* be right now. That, you can deal with. *Shoulds* only make you crazy. Don't be crazy.

You are not in charge of the actions of others, nor are you in control of the rotation of the earth, last week's audition, trends in the business, traffic in Los Angeles, or anything at all outside of you. You cannot change the past. You cannot predict the future. Regretting what should have been does not serve you today. Worrying about what might go wrong only distracts you from fully experiencing your career right now and choosing for yourself what's next for you. Today, all you can do is accept and embrace where you are and then step into an even brighter and more fulfilling tomorrow free of any *shoulds*.

Hey! While you're at it, don't *should* on anybody else either! As much as you would like to be in charge of the people around you, you just aren't. Believing or assuming that you are distracts you from the one person you can control. That person is you. Worrying about how hard your agent works on your behalf does not in any way bring your agent to more action. Wondering what a casting director thinks about you does not in any way change their opinion. You cannot control the thoughts or actions of anyone else, so do yourself a favor and stop behaving like you can.

My client, Candice, is a tremendous talent. Her chops are incredible and her career is currently on an upswing. A month ago, Candice actually brought a casting director to tears during her moving performance at an audition. Before the audition was even over, Candice already had a callback scheduled for the next day. Leaving the room, she was pretty sure she had this one in the bag. Though the callback went equally as well as the original audition, Candice didn't end up booking the job.

What the heck is that about? If a casting director literally melts into tears, shouldn't that mean that the job is yours? Evidently not, yet Candice spent hours mentally revisiting every moment of her auditions hoping to figure out what went wrong. Candice believed that this casting director *should* have hired her. This belief created tons of anxiety for Candice and in some way implied that Candice somehow had some sort of control over this casting director's mind. This example seems so obvious. Surely, Candice knows that she has no mind controlling powers. Yet, most people do this day after day. They *should* on others all the time! Think about it. How often have you experienced any of the following thoughts?

My agent should get me more auditions.
People should appreciate my hard work.
My roommate should wash his dishes once in a while.
My parents should support my career choice.
The industry should be easier.
Talent should be enough.
People shouldn't be rude.
Other actors shouldn't be so needy.
Managers shouldn't be so sketchy.
Acting class shouldn't be so expensive.
My wife should respect me.
Casting directors should be more accessible.

Regardless of how right or wrong these ideas appear, the truth is that you are not in charge of others. When you grab onto these *shoulds*, you easily become distracted by the business of other people rather than focused on your business. When you *should* others, you neglect yourself and that's just no way to live. *Should* only makes you powerless, so don't *should* on people. Trust that everyone is doing his or her job perfectly. Sometimes their job may rub you the wrong way or go against your master plan, which is okay. It doesn't mean they *should* change. It just means you disagree. Remember, trust is vital to *The Tao of Show Business.*

And another thing... when you find yourself judging or *should-ing*, take a look at how you can heed your own advice. The people in your life just mirror you. They're just reflecting your behavior, your perceptions, and your hang-ups. So when you judge others, it's just an opportunity to improve yourself.

A while ago, I felt like a number of people in my life were taking advantage of me. They weren't respecting my time or my boundaries and I was *should*-ing all over the place with thoughts like, "People *should* respect my time." After a few hours, I had to ask myself, "Okay, Dallas. Where are you not respecting your own boundaries?" Sure enough I realized that I was in a bad pattern of watching too much television and avoiding some pressing deadlines. I was showing myself no respect for my own time as a coach and teacher. As soon as I straightened myself out, wouldn't you know it—people began respecting my boundaries. Huh. What a coincidence!

If you feel like your agent *should* get you more auditions, you must look at how you can get yourself more auditions. If you believe people *should* appreciate your hard work, ask yourself where you might not be appreciating others. If your roommate isn't pulling his weight, examine where you can pick up your own slack. Where are your unwashed dishes, figuratively speaking? If you believe your parents *should* be more supportive, make an effort to be more supportive of their ideas and ambitions. If you feel that actors are too needy, seize this opportunity to practice your own independence. Casting directors *should* be more accessible, huh? If you believe that, you must then examine where in your life you can be more open and accessible.

It always comes back to you. When you *should* on others, it's a superb opportunity to improve, stretch and become a better version of you. Again, you cannot change people. You cannot dictate the lives of others, but you can use your *shoulds* as a tool to explore where you can improve your own life. So stop *should*-ing and start working on your own stuff. It'll restore your awareness of choice and bring your focus back to what you do have the ability to control – you.

DEVELOP THE TAO

Take a look at the Should Exercise in your
The Tao of Show Business Companion Workbook.

www.taoofshowbusiness.com/workbook.php

COMMITMENT IS KEY

YOUR CAREER JOURNEY LASTS A LIFETIME. IT'S WHAT you're here to do. If you want to truly master your own Tao of Show Business, you must commit to each and every step of your journey. You must commit to accomplishing the big picture. You must also commit to fully experiencing every step along your journey.

It wasn't long ago that you committed to a career as an actor. Do you remember when that was and how excited you were? Do you remember how fearlessly you behaved or how earnestly you sought out advice? Remember your very first film or your first time out onstage? Remember how thrilled you were to land auditions? Do you remember how exciting it was to mail out your headshots? How you truly knew that your dreams were about to become reality? Weren't those the days?

Today you know better. You've been around for a while and you understand how tough this business is, how difficult it is to get in the door, and how naïve you used to be when you first arrived in the big city.

Stop and think for a moment about how much easier your career pursuit was back when you didn't know any better. Think about how much fun you had, how hopeful you felt, and how easily you celebrated even the tiniest of victories.

You can return to that place of pure joy. You don't have to give up what you've learned along the way. Those lessons are invaluable. But don't lose your sense of wonder or your love of the little things. Hang on to that starry-eyed newbie who found joy in student film projects, mediocre theatre, and self-submissions. Infuse what you know today with how you felt long ago. Success in acting is still possible for you. All you have to do is continue to believe. All you have to do is pretend you don't know any better.

DEVELOP THE TAO

Pretend that you have everything to learn. Forget about past disappointments and renew your sense of wonderment about your acting career.

www.taoofshowbusiness.com/workbook.php

That Last Fifteen Percent

Steven Pressfield wrote what I think is one of the greatest books for artists. It's called *The War of Art* and it's a must read. Pressfield describes the many forms of resistance, including the resistance that shows up at the finish line.

Pressfield writes:

> *"Odysseus almost got home years before his actual homecoming. Ithaca was in sight, close enough that the sailors could see the smoke of their families' fires on shore. Odysseus was so certain he was safe, he actually lay down for a snooze. It was then that his men, believing there was gold in an ox-hide sack among their commander's possessions, snatched this prize and cut it open. The bag contained the adverse winds, which King Aeolus had bottled up for Odysseus when the wanderer had touched earlier at his blessed isle. The winds burst forth now in one mad blow, driving Odysseus' ships back across every league of ocean they had with*

such difficulty traversed, making him endure further trials and sufferings before, at last and alone, he reached home for good.

"The danger is greatest when the finish line is in sight. At this point, Resistance knows we're about to beat it. It hits the panic button. It marshals one last assault and slams us with everything it's got.

The professional must be alert for this counterattack. Be wary at the end. Don't open that bag of wind."

Do you often struggle to finish projects? Do you lose focus when you're about to complete a task? Do you begin with fervor and excitement, yet lose steam just before you finish? On your journey to acting success, you must persevere through bumps in the road. You must be willing to finish what you start. You must follow through and resist the urge to quit or coast to the finish line. You must bring the same level of passion and excitement to the last fifteen percent of a project that you do when you begin something new.

Don't be an 85 percenter. Don't be the actor who can't seem to get things done. Set yourself up for success by committing to the big picture and following through even when things get icky, foggy, or unsexy. If you want to achieve your greatest potential, you must force yourself to focus on the end result and ensure that you'll finally cross that finish line. Commit to the process, so you can finish what you start.

Commit to the End Result

While you're building industry relationships, film credits, and confidence, it's easy to mistake every opportunity as the right opportunity. I am in no way opposed to actors doing free work. What a great way to collect demo reel footage, practice working on a set, and collaborate with talented emerging filmmakers. Free work is often good work. But you do not have to say yes to every job that comes your way. I also understand that before you sign with a top agent at CAA or ICM, you'll probably work with a handful of B and C level agents while you build your résumé. That's the way it goes and it's all right by me. But just any agent or manager will not do. You deserve the right people during every phase of your career.

My workshop student named Ruby secured herself a manager meeting through the referral of a fellow classmate. This manager represented other actors with decent credits and seemed to be a perfect fit for Ruby.

The day of the meeting, Ruby arrived at the manager's home right on time. She was excited and ready to strut her stuff. Upon entering the home, Ruby was surprised to see the place in complete disarray. The place was a mess with dirty dishes everywhere, dust on every surface, and a general stink in the air. Mr. Manager directed Ruby to his office, which also served as his bedroom. Ruby sat on this man's unmade bed while he spent the next twenty-or-so minutes berating her.

Ruby left the meeting feeling horrible about her appearance, her talent, and her future in the industry. She hated this manager. She thought he was a real jerk. Yet, Ruby decided that if this manager offered her a contract, she'd take it. He did have a reputation, right? He did get his clients work, after all. Surely, he knew more than she did about how to make it in show business…

You're probably thinking that Ruby is crazy for even considering working with such a horrible person. Yet, so many actors forfeit their own opinions or interests to the ideas of so-called experts in the business. Ruby's story is just an exaggerated version of situations that play out day after day in Hollywood. Actors stop sticking up for themselves in hopes of snagging a break. Actors believe that they must settle for whatever opportunities come their way, regardless of what their guts tell them. Actors say yes to things that don't fit into their long-term vision, even a little bit.

Yes, there is such a thing as paying your dues. Yes, sometimes you have to give a little to get a little. Sure, you need to work for free sometimes, and you'll have to compromise, cooperate, and be flexible while you build your team. But saying "no" to things that do not jive with you means saying "yes" to something better.

My client, Tilda, had no extra time to think straight let alone time to take on extra projects. Tilda spent most of her time driving around from audition to table reading, to film shoot and back again. She was under-rested and unfocused. But Tilda was working, so she felt that she had no right to complain.

The trouble was that the majority of the work Tilda agreed to was unpaid work. Tilda had a résumé filled with film and television credits. She's been a working actor for over a decade, yet she couldn't seem to break through her plateau into series-regular status. Still, Tilda performed in student films and other time-consuming projects that did not reflect where she wanted to take her career.

Tilda believed that she had to say "yes" to each and every job that came her way. She was scared to miss out if she said "no." Tilda couldn't see the connection between the work she agreed to and the work that eluded her.

You see, Tilda was so busy doing the same old work, that there was no room in her career for better jobs. If you want to create new results, you must first make room for those things to appear. You've got to set boundaries and create incredible standards for the work you do, the people you work with, and the career you create. If you don't, you can expect more of the same old thing.

Reject the Myth of the Starving Artist

In order to get what you really want, you must commit to taking consistent, persistent, and inspired action for your career. But there's more to it than that. Remember that the Tao is all about living a harmonious life. Some people would like to believe that nothing else exists in the world outside of their careers. It's just not true.

Beware of the myth of the starving artist. It isn't true and it doesn't apply to you when you live *The Tao of Show Business*. Hard work is great and absolutely necessary to succeed in this business. But true success comes when you give the same level of love, attention and effort to all aspects of your life. When you commit fully to everything that matters, you are a success. When you respect your personal life as much as your professional life, you are a success. When you put attention on your finances today rather than wait for that big paycheck, you are a success. When you celebrate the little victories as much as the big ones, you are a success.

Jenna Fischer, that really funny actress who plays Pam on *The Office*, wrote an incredible blog that you must read. You can find it in its entirety at www.myspace.com/pambeesley. In it, she addresses so many myths, tricks, and tips for every actor in Hollywood.

Touching on commitment, Fischer wrote "Create a family for yourself of creative, supportive people. And don't stop your personal life for your career. I know a lot of people that wait to do things —visit family, friends, have relationships, get married—because they are waiting until they "make it." Or, they don't go to a friend's wedding because they might "miss something." Life is too short and it's not worth it in the end. I always took off and did that stuff and it turned out fine. I was often anxious and worried in the process but I did it. I believe that in order for my professional life to move forward, I have to keep my personal life moving forward as well."

Let go of your belief in the starving artist myth. Yeah, we've all seen *Rent* and though there is something noble or even admirable about suffering for the sake of your art, the reality of it is not so good. Not only is it not so good, but it's also the tougher way to live. You must really choose suffering, lack and discomfort in order to experience it. There's an easier way and that way is the Tao.

To live *The Tao of Show Business* means to live in harmony with your career whether you're waiting tables or winning Oscars. There is nothing harmonious about bouncing checks, missing family trips, struggling to make ends meet, and just being broke and unhappy. You are an actor because acting fulfills you. There is nothing fulfilling about waiting around to book your series before you enjoy your life. That is the opposite of fulfillment. You are an actor because you want to inspire people. There is nothing inspired about working with a jerk-of-a-manager just because it's better to have somebody than nobody. That's not the way it works and it doesn't have to be your story.

This business is only as crazy as you want it to be. It's your choice. Though it's essential that you commit to your long-term success as an actor, you must also commit to living a balanced and fulfilled life today. It's a lot easier to treat yourself like a starving artist than to behave like the genius you know you are. It's a lot safer to play small, struggle and suffer than it is to make bold choices and change some lives with the work you deliver. That's for sure.

The way you do anything directly reflects and affects the way you do everything. Respect your career, but don't neglect your finances, your personal life, or your day-to-day enjoyment. Life is way too short to suffer on your way to success. Now is the time to master the habits of living a balanced and fulfilled life. This framework will influence your life after you "make it."

WHAT ARE YOU WAITING FOR?

THE ONLY THING STANDING BETWEEN YOU AND THE career of your dreams is time. So how will you choose to spend your time? When you practice *The Tao of Show Business,* your ultimate dreams will one day become a reality. Why can't today be that day? Nothing at all prevents you from behaving as though your goals are already accomplished. Enjoy the journey and treat yourself as though you are already the award winning, successful, inspiring actor that you dream of becoming. The more willing you are to live this way, the more easily and quickly your vision will unfold right before your eyes. These results will not surprise you because you'll already be living as though you have these things and so much more.

Henry Ford once said, "Whether you think you can , or think you can't, you are usually right." It's true for your career as well. Do you think it's possible to live a successful and fulfilling life as a thriving artist right now? Or do you think it's too much work? Either way, you're right, so pick the perspective that serves you. As hokey as it may sound, living as though you've already made it is the most powerful thing you can do. Not only will it allow you to easily get where you want to be, but it'll make getting there a heck of a lot more enjoyable.

You know everything you need to know right now to take the next step for your acting career. You always have. When will you do it? When will you live your Tao?

Now is the time to tap into your purpose and use that vision to propel you forward. Now is the time to live the life you've always imagined. You know your Tao. Let it lead you to that purpose. Let

it show you the way.

Now is the time to declare your goals to the people around you and to invite them to participate in your path to success. Collaborate and create the projects you dream of today. Now is the time. Don't wait to share your talents with the world and to shine your light brightly. Don't shy away from the success that is yours.

Now is the time to take inspired action and live each day without regret or hesitation. Do those things that inspire you most and do them consistently. Now is the time to embrace your mistakes so you can improve your craft, expand your business, and create lasting change in your life. Now is the time to let go of any need to control, to know everything, or to be perfect. Now is the time to live a little dangerously, to step into the future that awaits you and to live your Tao.

Go ahead and take that next step. Now is the time to master *The Tao of Show Business.* It's up to you. What are you waiting for?

DEVELOP THE TAO

Don't let the day go by without doing something for your acting career! Set this book down, stand up, and take action. Don't wait. Don't think. Just move.

www.taoofshowbusiness.com/workbook.php

An Invitation:

BECOME A THRIVING ARTIST

Join the Thriving Artist Circle Free for 30 Days.

I invite you to thrive today as an artist and succeed as an actor. I want you to continue to learn, grow and master your own *Tao of Show Business.* Put what you've learned in this book into action. You can generate new results, follow through, and finally live the career of your dreams when you join the Thriving Artist Circle.

The Thriving Artist Circle is your one-stop resource for everything you need to enjoy a purpose-driven and inspired life along with the incredible success you desire and deserve.

The Thriving Artist Circle connects actors and artists to practical tips, tools and strategies necessary to achieve greatness in your career and balance in your life.

This monthly membership program is guaranteed to help you focus on your priorities, connect you to your purpose, maintain consistent action and stay inspired along your journey.

I know you'll love it, so the first month's on me. Get your free 30-day membership now.

www.thrivingartistcircle.com

See ya there!

About The Author:

Dallas Travers is an IPEC certified Creative Career Coach, motivational speaker, and President of Sage Creative, Inc. Infusing practical knowledge with inspired ideas, she has helped hundreds of actors generate remarkable personal and professional breakthroughs. She provides lectures, training, and private coaching for actors, writers, and creative entrepreneurs across the globe.

In 2001, Dallas founded Sage Creative, Inc., an innovative consulting firm for actors, artists and other creative entrepreneurs. Since then, she has worked to counteract the many myths and stumbling blocks in the business by creating an environment where actors can control their own careers.

During her time at Sage, Dallas noticed that her clients shared the same questions about career mastery, confidence, and basic marketing and management skills. So, she began to conduct workshops to address these very issues. Dallas soon fell in love with teaching and has continued to motivate actors and artists throughout the country at various workshops and events.

In the summer of 2008, Dallas released the acclaimed educational CD, *Living Mantras: Mastering the Art of Positive Speaking*. This CD introduces the simple yet transformative practice of consciously asking empowering questions in order produce new results in your career as well as your life. Dallas is also a contributing author to the award-winning anthology, *Conscious Entrepreneurs*, compiled by Christine Kloser.

Touted as one of the leading career coaches in the entertainment industry, Dallas Travers teaches actors and artists the career and life skills that are often overlooked in traditional training programs.

Dallas also practices what she preaches. She continually educates herself, sets and meets new career goals, and works to add value to the lives of everyone she meets. Dallas enjoys life in Los Angeles, CA where she lives with her husband and two dogs.

Connect with Dallas at: www.dallastravers.com